"Live your life with p...

UNLEASH THE MAGNET IN YOU

THE ULTIMATE CHALLENGE

Don Xavier

iUniverse, Inc.

New York   Bloomington

Unleash the Magnet in You

Credits: Written by Don Xavier; book design by Don Xavier and Rosilda Xavier; edited by Shelden Smollan and Rosilda Xavier Cover design by Rosilda Xavier; photography by Jim Dawson, Fotowork: www.fotowork.ca

Eduardo Martins, Timevision Photography Inc.:
www.timevisionphoto.ca

Contact: Don Xavier, Agroma Publishing Inc.: 2794 Rainbow Crescent, Mississauga, ON L5L 5W1; toll free: 866-396-5445, ext. 225, or direct: 416-562-9780 or e-mail: dxavier@donxavier.ca

W W W . D O N X A V I E R . C O M

iUniverse books may be ordered through booksellers or by contacting:

iUniverse
1663 Liberty Drive
Bloomington, IN 47403
www.iuniverse.com
1-800-Authors (1-800-288-4677)

ISBN: 978-1-4502-6737-3 (sc)
ISBN: 978-1-4502-6738-0 (ebk)

Printed in the United States of America
iUniverse rev. date: 10/15/2010

YES
YES
YES

Unleash the Triangle Principles

Dedications

To three magnificent people: my mother, Maria Rosilda Lopes; my grandmother Etelvina Lopes; and my father, Arnaldo Monteiro Xavier. I thank you for giving me a strong soul; a good heart, body, and mind; and the commitment to bravery, perseverance, determination, and strong work ethics.

Special dedication in memory of
My two very special Uncles:
Adelino Lopes (*Titio*)
and
Manuel Cardoso (*Tio Naio*)

God Bless and R.I.P.

Table of Contents

Acknowledgments

I would like to acknowledge the two amazing women in my life: my wife, Maria Xavier, and my daughter, Rosilda Xavier. The two of you represent the true definition of strength, consistency, and persistency for unconditionally supporting me and for continuing your high level of enthusiasm and belief in my work for the past twenty-plus years. I feel so blessed to have you both in my life; you mean the world to me, and I love you unconditionally.

I would also like to extend my sincere thank you to the following individuals for playing a positive role in my life: Alirio Xavier, Ernesto Xavier, Olavo Xavier, Maria (*Rigala*) Xavier-Carvalho, Joaquina Xavier, Adriano Carvalho, Benvindo Carvalho, Domingos Xavier, Irlando Barros, Manuel Barros, Jose Barros, Ilda Lopes, Lucilia Carvalho, Maria Xavier (*mulher di Domingos*), Nana Xavier, Luluxa Xavier, Fefa Xavier (*di tio Alirio*), Laura Pina Tavares (*nha madrinha*), Arlindo Monteiro Xavier (*nha padrinho*), Alfredo (*Fefe*) Barros, Ricardo Pina Tavares, Domingos and Aninha De Pina, Ana (*Idite*) Goncalves, Manuel (*Nene*) Baptista, Eulanda Baptista, Ana Julia Sanca, George Fidalgo (*RIP*) and also to all my brothers and sisters and all my great brothers and sisters in-law.

Antonio Cesar, Eduardo Martins, Jim Dawson, Sam Madio, Ramiro Mendes, Joao Domingos Mendes, Gerry Mudge, Augusto Veiga, Jorge (*Pimpa*) Martins, Adolfo (*Antoni di Olavo*) Cardoso, Adao Brito, Gabriel

Nicoletti, Dimingo Dindin, Joao P. Carvalho (*J*), Faustino Monteiro, Ferro Gaita, Sabrina Loessl, Aidas Batura, Leandro Fortes, Ed Andrade, Shelden Smollan, Geoffrey Charlton, and (*Edy*) João Augusto Mendes Monteiro—thanks for building our dream beach home.

Thank you to the following promoters:

- Alex Nicholson and Tom Miller
- www.pro-seminars.com
- Shelden Smollan
- www.crosswalkinsurance.com
- www.topadvisorforum.com

Thank you to all the television, newspapers, magazines, Web sites, and radio stations that promoted my work, including:

- Valdir Alves, (*Cabo Video*)
- Claudio Fonseca (www.manduco.net)
- Osvaldo Reis (www.cvmusicworld.com)
- www.versatilefinancial.com
- www.caboverdeonline.com
- www.capeverdeanart.com
- Alberto Pina (www.forcv.com)

Thank you to all the companies that have hired me to speak at their events.

In addition, it is with great pleasure that I thank all the people who have supported me by attending my seminars and workshops and buying my books online.

Introduction

Let me begin by saying that this book has been written and designed to assist you in taking total control as well as responsibility for your success. It focuses on the full behavior cycles that will allow you to attract the people you meet and talk to by mastering entrepreneurial and life skills that will remain valid throughout your lifetime. This book is going to assist you in turning *no, no, no* into *yes, yes, yes* in your life and business! You will learn that you can achieve your highest goals and objectives when you commit yourself to self-education, training, implementation, and hard work.

Develop a plan and hold yourself accountable for the writing of your personal storybook. You will have a clear picture in attaining your full potential by utilizing a role model, mastering the Laws of the 4k's *(from my book Motivational Cycles to Successful Selling),* and unleashing the magnet within you. The many different sections of this book will demonstrate the power you possess in controlling your future success in your life and business.

You will discover that when you believe, you shall receive. You can shape your destiny because life is about creating yourself. Your actions today will determine your outcome tomorrow. So how will you act today?

You have nothing to lose and will only gain when you take the opportunity and master the principles in *Unleash the Magnet in You: The Ultimate Challenge*! With a positive mental attitude and the drive to take action, you can achieve your ultimate goals and objectives.

Live your life with passion; you can make a difference when you believe and want something badly enough, helping yourself and others along the way.

Understand that The Ultimate Challenge solely depends on the decisions we make and the actions we take. It is so important that our successes and failures are based on the decisions we make, the level of actions we take, and how big we dream.

Dream big and you shall have a big reality!

Don Xavier

IN THE BEGINNING

In the Beginning

When I began writing this book, I recalled watching a television program on which a singer mentioned that in his new comeback show, he was going to sing the songs his fans wanted him to sing. His comments gave me an idea, and I started thinking about the topic of this book. I decided to write this book about the subjects my supporters would want me to write about. They would want me to write a book that would help them with ideas on how to become the very best they can be.

The purpose of this book is to develop great ideas. It is about everlasting principles used by successful individuals throughout history. Since 1994, I have studied the behavior of these successful individuals, and I have committed myself to implementing these principles in my own life and business. The success that I now enjoy is the result of religiously applying these principles day in and day out.

It came to me early in my career that I could not buy success; I had to earn it with hard work and dedication. I realized that I had to effectively learn the principles and apply them in order to achieve a certain level of success. The more I applied, the more I enjoyed it—and the more I got in return. The rewards are all worth it, and they continue to get better and better as I master the methods of applying the principles I have summed up in *Unleash the Magnet in You*.

Mr. Warren Buffett said, "To invest successfully over a lifetime does not require a stratospheric IQ, unusual business insight, or inside information. What's needed is a sound intellectual framework for decisions and the ability to keep emotions from corroding that framework."

Interpret the above quotation by changing the first three words so it reads as follows: "[To be successful] over a lifetime does not require a stratospheric IQ, unusual business insight, or inside information. What's needed is a sound intellectual framework for decisions and the ability to keep emotions from corroding that framework."

In my walk of life, I have come to understand that successful people deal with their businesses, lives, and finances in a specific manner. I have analyzed this approach and summarized five tried and true principles, which I have identified as The Five Principles for creating a successful future.

The Five Principles:

> **Principle #1** – Have a specific framework.
> **Principle #2** – Utilize other people's expertise.
> **Principle #3** – Utilize other people's capital.
> **Principle #4** – Compensate yourself first.
> **Principle #5** – Take a long-term approach.

I understand that while these principles are simple, they may not be easy to fully apply. This is the sole reason why this book is subtitled *The Ultimate Challenge*. To assist you in learning the powerful principles of how to *Unleash the Magnet in You*, I have simplified this book and organized it into sections.

Every success begins with a first step toward your goals. By following these principles, one step at a time and one day at the time, you will see that you too can begin to achieve your goals and success in your life and business.

Keep in mind that the decisions we make and the actions we take make all the difference in our lives and business. I strongly believe that these principles can be applied in our lives and business and achieve amazing success as long as we understand and possess the know-how to unleash the magnet within ourselves. Once you clearly understand and apply the true meaning of *Unleash the Magnet in You*, I'm convinced that you will enjoy the results. Understanding will help the process; you will reap the benefits and see a clear path to a great future.

Clearly understanding the principles herein will require a change in lifestyle and a personal transformation in order to create new opportunities. It's then that you will need to think about and decide who you want to be, and where you want to take your life and business. Discover what really matters to you and create your brightest possible future.

So many individuals go through their entire lives without ever having a clear picture of who they are and where they come from in order to discover who they want to be. Before you can plan for where you are going, you must first know where you are.

Once you have a clear picture of the person you are today, you can take action on your dreams of who you want to be. With education, training, implementation, hard work, and following the guidance of people you respect, you can start achieving your dreams, goals, and wants, one step at a time.

You will also need to focus on perfecting every aspect of your life and business, even if you need to seek out individuals who can teach you and provide you with sound advice. *Unleash the Magnet in You* can help you identify your own abilities in order to create an idealistic and realistic plan for achieving your goals. By writing this book, my goal is to help you go away with a sense of purpose and understanding of what you need to do in order to unleash the magnet within you. When I help you unleash your inner magnet in order to turn your dreams into a reality, then I will have succeeded.

Are you the type of individual who loves to win time and time again? If the answer is yes, then let me ask another question: Are you the type of individual who is prepared to educate, learn, and implement until you win, even if it hurts? If so, that is great because you become what you think about and act upon! There is absolutely nothing more exciting than having a goal and setting out to achieve it with confidence and determination. It doesn't mean that it's going to be easy, because nothing worthwhile is ever easy. However, when you have a clear vision for the kind of life you want for yourself and you have the passion to follow that vision, the sky is the limit for you.

Let's get started!

Unleash the Magnet in You

Don Xavier

THE   MIND
+
THE   ACTION
=
THE   RESULTS

Chapter One

You've heard the saying "A mind is a terrible thing to waste." And if you're familiar with my work, then you know that I believe in my own saying about the mind: *You can become whatever it is you think about and act upon!*

Our level of success has been proven repeatedly that the end result of anything largely depends on how we influence our minds to carry out a task. When you condition your mind to achieve positive results, that's what you will receive. When you condition your mind to achieve negative results, that's what you'll receive. The mind is so powerful that it's invisible.

I'll give you an example: I once knew a young man who everyone thought was mentally challenged mainly because of his physical difficulties. This individual utilized his mind to the fullest. Personally, I found him simply amazing. People would tell him a specific date in the future, and he would tell them exactly what day of the week that date would fall on.

Some people believe that our minds and our brains are one of the same; however, others believe this is incorrect. The brain is a physical object that can be seen with the naked eye. The mind is not a physical object. It cannot be seen with the naked eye, unlike the brain, which can be seen, photographed, or even repaired by surgery.

Allegedly, nothing within our bodies can be identified as being our minds because our bodies and minds are different entities. The mind is often used to refer principally to the thought processes of reason. Subjectively, the mind manifests itself as a flow of consciousness.

If you check the dictionary or search the Internet, you will find many different meanings of the word "mind." This is my own definition and understanding of the mind, and how I have utilized my mind along with taking actions in order to achieve the results I want in my life and business.

While I said that the mind is invisible, taking action is visible. Once you have convinced your mind that you have a particular vision or goal, prepare to take action. Remember that nothing happens overnight. Take it one step at a time and keep in mind that the number one thing that keeps people from getting what they truly want out of life is not *taking action*, which is the ultimate challenge.

It's important that you program your mind for unlimited success. Success won't happen automatically by any means. Each day, you must choose to live your life with an attitude that expects incredible and fascinating things to happen.

You must set your mind and sustain it on the higher goals. When your goals are higher, you will achieve higher results. When you open your eyes in the morning, the first thing you must have is thinking time in order to set your mind on the right path. You may want to have a special saying like, "This is going to be a fantastic day," or if you're like me, you can say, "This is going to be a yes-yes-yes day!"

Expect the unexpected: for example, getting all green lights driving to work, finding a parking space wherever you go, and people going out of their way for you. Be prepared to smile at everyone you meet, and they will do the same for you.

However, don't be surprised if you don't get all green lights driving to work, or you don't find the closest parking space, or if not everyone goes out of the way for you. What is important is that you maintain focus and keep your mind positive. Expect an abundance of opportunities to come to you in every aspect of your life.

Let me give you another example. When I had the vision of writing my first book, I knew little beyond having the dream, the idea, of writing a book … as well as a positive mental attitude. Therefore, I began to do research, took courses on writing, read books and magazines, attended workshops, and listened to educational CDs and cassettes. Once I had a clearer picture of how to begin writing a book, I strategized my goal and plan of action for writing my first book.

Once you have acquired the knowledge and the vision in your mind, and sent the message to your brain, the brain tells the body to take action, and you can then begin taking action with confidence.

> *Don't settle for whatever; tell your mind that you deserve the very best, write down your action plan, follow it step by step, one day at the time, and you are guaranteed to produce amazing results.*

It doesn't really matter what your vision is. You can accomplish it by psychologically taking control of your own being. Focus on taking action. Be proud of yourself and make the most of your life.

The way you take control of your vision is the way which will position you on top of your priorities in order to accomplish amazing things without making excuses and help you kick up your zest for life. Result and motive are what keep us going. When you enjoy what you do and want to achieve extraordinary results, then you must identify ways to improve your performance and create a strategy that will put you ahead of your competitors.

Remain extremely focused and always remember that obstacles are the things we see the minute we take our eyes off our goals and lose focus.

Most people are easily distracted by our surroundings and the company we keep. Make sure you are surrounded by positive people who will only motivate and support your visions and goals. I've been known to tell people, "If you don't have anything positive to say to me, please don't say anything at all." I've also been known to say, "Show me your friends and I will tell you about you."

Life should be about making the choices you want and not about some options that someone else has given you. Condition your mind to accept only the very best for yourself; shake off mediocrity, and demand a life of passion. Like attracts like, and once you possess a supercharged lifestyle, you will begin to attract other like-minded individuals to you. It's important to focus on people, not things, and remember that your mind will manifest itself subjectively as a stream of consciousness.

Our mind power is more than just about positive thinking. Once you realize that the power of your thoughts and beliefs create reality, then you will start to pay close attention to the thoughts you are thinking, powered by the actions you take.

You can begin to direct the awesome power of your mind and subconscious mind to create the beautiful life you want and deserve. Once you have mastered and unleashed your subconscious mind power, this will help you develop the personal power that you already possess to create your success and fulfillment in life.

We talked about the mind and action; now let's look at the results. Seeing results will keep you motivated to continue working on whatever it is you're doing until you achieve your ultimate goal.

One of the main goals people have is losing weight. Imagine being on a weight loss program and not losing any weight. This can be devastating, as it is not the result you are hoping for. On the other hand, when you begin to notice weight loss, the results make you feel good and encourage you to move forward.

Being results oriented is great because it motivates you to continue working on your endeavors. The initial results will give you validation that you are heading in the right direction toward your goals. Never procrastinate. Make certain that you don't put off until tomorrow the things that you can do today. Start taking action right now; even though your initial results may be minimal, you will be motivated to continue with your actions.

Before you move forward to the next section of this book, stop and make a clear personal commitment as to how you're going to allow the information in this book to make a difference in your life. Make a personal decision that you will immediately implement the information and ideas in your life and your business.

Keep in mind that the Mind + the Action = the Results.

When you have imagination you can write history. *Don Xavier*

B E C O M E   A
P E O P L E
M A G N E T

Y E S !
Y E S !   Y E S !

Chapter Two

As a child growing up in Cape Verde Island, magnets fascinated to me. I kept on thinking, *What if humans could possess such a force in attracting people to one another the same way magnets do?*

I found it amazing watching this mysterious invisible force pulling metals. It made me conjure up humorous images of magical powers emanating from the magnets. Many people must wonder exactly what a magnet is. According to the Universe Today's website's definition: *A magnet is any material that possesses a magnetic field. This field exerts forces on any ferromagnetic material within its vicinity.*

It is human nature that individuals are not attracted to all other individuals. Like a magnet, not all metals are attracted to magnets. For example, silver, gold, copper, and aluminum are considered non-ferromagnetic metals and are therefore not attracted to magnets.

What I'm saying is that even though true people magnetizers should attract everyone they meet and talk to, you will find that there will be people that you won't be able to attract no matter what you do. Some people will be attracted, and some people won't. So what? Next! Move on.

Success can be like a magnetic power! You are a magnet attracting everything into your life through the signals you are emitting with your thoughts, behavior, and feelings. When you gain knowledge, overcome the resistance, and take action, your magnetism will create ripples through the lives of most people you meet and talk to.

Picture yourself and everything you do as the center of your world. You have to believe that in order to become a people magnet, you must first understand yourself, study yourself, accept yourself, and fall in love with yourself to drive others to fall in love with you. The bottom line is, people will like and love you more when you like and love yourself.

You hold the power to decide who you want to be, what life you want to live, and what dreams you want to make a reality. Put your dreams in the spotlight, visualize your achievement, and prioritize your values.

When you visualize it, you will magnetize it, and with faith and action, it will materialize. When you are great, the whole world should know you are great! Make some noise about yourself and your business. If you don't make noise, the result is mediocrity. I believe that in order to become a super people magnet each and every day, you must focus on making a difference in the lives of each and every person you meet and talk to. Think about every step you take and every smile you give, thinking about the effects they will have on other people's lives. A real smile is priceless; therefore, give one to everyone you meet and talk to, and in return you will receive an endless chain of real smiles to brighten your day.

Becoming a people magnet is simple; it's all about having a clear understanding of the meaning and the simple actions you must take in your daily life. If you're a shy or reserved individual, becoming a magnet can be a slight challenge, but it's definitely not impossible. Begin by taking tiny steps. Start talking and smiling with your neighbors, your co-workers, people in elevators, people in the mall, the postman, the waste collector, etc. Before you know, others will start talking and smiling to you, and you will begin to feel comfortable enough to always smile and start a conversation with confidence. The key is to decide to make a change and take action.

It's possible that you have wondered what makes some people so magnetic—and wondered how you can become a people magnet too. I believe the reason certain people seem to have the magnetic ability to draw others toward them may not be a special gift after all; it may just be a quality available to all of us.

During my career, I have been fascinated by watching people interact with other people or just go about their daily business, oblivious to anything or anyone else around them. This is how I began to master the secret to becoming a people magnet.

Don't misunderstand me. The secret of how to become a people magnet is not something that only I know or have magically discovered. I have no doubt that you too most certainly know and understand why some people are so magnetic.

One of the ways to become a people magnet is by observing other people you know who seem to be so magnetic and paying close attention to how they act and how they carry themselves around other people … and then do the same.

Over the years, I have invested quality time examining and studying the behavior of many people who are magnets in my social circle and others that are better known to the general public. The interesting thing is that all people who are magnets seem to have a similar trait, and that is genuine self-confidence. I literally mean *genuine*—not fake, not artificial, and not a form of confidence that they only display when others are watching. I'm referring to an authentic confidence that is unmistakably genuine in all circumstances. I'm almost certain that this is their lifestyle, and that they live by it devotedly.

For example, one individual I have known for several years demonstrates genuine self-confidence with his consistent behavior, transparency, appearance, sense of humour, and stability in his personal life. When I talked to his wife, she mentioned how happy she was, crediting him with being a wonderful husband and telling how much he contributed around the house.

You can do this too, just by following the ideas I've given you. Don't try to reinvent the wheel; just take the one that is already invented and personalize it (don't copy) and live it.

The key is to unconditionally love yourself, both the good and the bad, and people will see through that and magnetize to you. This is proven without a doubt to be the truth.

The main reason there seems to be so few people magnets amongst us is because too many people are worried about what others think of them instead of being their own true selves. It is only when you decide to get past the insecurity of worrying about what others think about you, and you are completely free to be your true self to do whatever it is you want in life—then in the process, you will become a people magnet.

Our lives are dependent upon other people, as we are all interrelated. Therefore, the most powerful ability you can ever have is being able to deal with people. It is an absolute necessity to learn how to deal with people effectively and become a people magnet. Say yes to taking action on becoming a people magnet and reap the rewards of loving and being loved.

I reiterate: Every section of this book will talk about the importance of conditioning our minds and sending information to our brains to eventually tell our bodies to take action, which is the ultimate challenge.

You deserve to live your very best life now, so decide to take action and make it happen!

As we move on to the next section of the book, it's important for you to remember that everything must always happen in your mind before it can ever happen in your life.

When you *visualize* it
you will *magnetize* it
and it will *materialize*.

CHAPTER THREE

BECOME A
" M A V E N "

Chapter Three

For the most part, Unleash the Magnet in You is about being a maven. You may be wondering what being a maven entails, and why anyone would want to be a maven.

Following my live presentations, people who remember or wrote down the word maven frequently approach me with the magical question: "So, Don, what is a maven?"

According to Wikipedia*: A maven is someone who is a trusted professional in a particular field and who seeks to pass his or her knowledge on to others. A maven is an expert.*

The word *maven* comes from the Yiddish, via Hebrew, and means one who understands, based on an accumulation of knowledge. A maven is knowledgeable, lives by a certain philosophy, and has a strategy to make his projects a simple format. Once you have familiarized yourself with this strategy, making decisions will be easy.

Mavens are the kinds of people who create awareness in their absence. They decide which types of individuals they want to populate their lives and businesses with. Usually this decision is based on individuals who are smart, energetic, hands-on, creative, passionate, motivated, focused and like-minded.

Mavens usually bulletproof themselves by differentiating and living as true mavens. They are focused on walking the talk, are extremely knowledgeable in their business, have a transparent lifestyle, self brand, know how to unleash the magnet within themselves, transfer their knowledge and enthusiasm to others, and take action.

Mavens have a process that makes their efforts easy and simple, therefore allowing themselves to *differentiate* and win: providing a uniform system, quality information, guidelines for best practice, and transparency.

Don't leave your life and career to chance. Become an expert through experience and take control of your emotions. Becoming a maven doesn't need to be complicated. Begin by having high expectations for yourself, guided by strong principles. By knowing your purpose, you can take your life and business to an everlasting higher level.

Many people have said, "If you stand for nothing, you will fall for everything." In this book, you will need to pay close attention to the chapter "The Principles of Knowing You." Therein, you will learn how to create a uniform system in order to differentiate yourself and make a strong impact on your life and business.

Mavens realize that greatness lies not in being strong, but in the right use of strength. They allocate a certain amount of time daily to think. They have found that being a maven is one of the shortest and surest ways to achieve success. It definitely cuts down on the costly mistakes, and it makes their work and life more interesting and less tiring.

They maintain enthusiasm by believing that enthusiasm is an excellent lubricant for their minds. Mavens take every *no* as a sign and a step toward getting closer to hearing *yes*. They discuss opportunities instead of problems. In most cases, mavens are entrepreneurs, and they will work fifteen hours a day for themselves just to avoid having to work eight hours a day for someone else.

Mavens go through problems instead of going around them because they know that the solution to most or all problems lies within the problem itself. They also believe that there are no impossible dreams, just impatient people, knowing that it takes time, dedication, and hard work to succeed. And they know that success is the reward for taking enough time to do something well for themselves and others.

Mavens always take time to learn, train, and implement knowledge in their life and business. They take the road less traveled because they clearly know that the position of being the same is taken by others.

To be a maven you must be an individual who is hungry about knowledge and who truly wants to have more success in your life and business. To accomplish this, all you need to do is develop a winning attitude and the expectation for success—and then *act* upon it. You are absolutely right if you're thinking that this process is simple, however not easy—because you must first change the way you think in order to change the way you live. Once that is done, it's that easy.

Let me prove a point to you in a short exercise. Close your eyes for a moment. Clear your mind and do the following:

- Think happy thoughts and you will begin to *feel* happy!
- The next time you're sitting beside someone, spontaneously turn to that person with a huge smile on your face and energetically say, "Hi, how are you?"

With the second bullet point, two things can happen. The person next to you can immediately start thinking you're crazy … or turn to you with the same level of enthusiasm. Of course, we must anticipate the latter happening. You can always change the environment around you just by changing the way you speak and think. Whatever it is you want, you can *magnetize* it to you just by unleashing the magnet within you.

Being a maven is not something you can touch or taste; it must be a lifestyle. A maven is not gender specific. It is, I believe, accomplishment specific. A maven is someone who is a master in any field. Therefore, according to that definition, you can be a maven if you are knowledgeable in your own particular field and are willing to share that knowledge with others.

So why would anyone want to be a maven? In our generation, it has become clear that individuals want to deal with people who are masters of their craft, and the more you know, the more you are able to share with others.

Every day we are given a luxury of twenty-four hours or … 1,440 minutes. This is one of the few gifts in the universe that we receive complimentary. Even if we had all the money in the world, we wouldn't be able to buy an additional hour. The question is, what will you do with this priceless treasure? Mavens will always remember that they must use it effectively, as this gift is only given once, and once wasted, we will never get it back again. Take action to become a maven.

> "A maven is someone who is a trusted professional in a particular field, and who seeks to pass his or her knowledge on to others."

CHAPTER
FOUR

THREE BASIC
PRINCIPLES
FOR
SUCCESS

Chapter Four

The Basic Principles for Success are essential. After investing years of my treasured time studying the behavior of successful people, my observation and analysis has been that all the successful individuals I studied had one main quality in common: they all devotedly applied the Basic Principles for Success in their lives and businesses.

As a speaker, I give presentations to thousands of successful leaders each year who want to become even better at what they do. They are key executives and management for major companies. They are intelligent, dedicated, determined, motivated, and goal oriented. They are committed to their success and the success of their companies, associates and peers. They possess high levels of personal integrity, innovation, and initiative. Most are financially independent or working toward it. They are definitely not working because they must; they are working simply because they want to meet their goals. These are individuals who live by the Basic Principles of Success in their lives and businesses, and they are the ideal people to be principle number one.

Principle #1: You must recognize a **Role Model**.

My idea of a true role model is an individual who possess the qualities that I dream of having. They are individuals who have affected me in ways that make me yearn to be a superior individual and to advocate for me and my goals and take leadership on the issues that I believe in.

I've often found that we don't clearly recognize our proper role models until we have personally noticed our own personal desires, plans, and progress and have a clearer picture of who we want to be. When identifying a role model, it is preferable that you choose someone who is in a similar field as you, although that's not completely necessary as long as you're following the basic principles. Some of the qualities the role model should possess are being an outstanding individual who possesses great character, strong values, and a winning attitude. The role model should also be a leader, an inspirational individual who has had measurable success.

Principle #2: Ask the role model for his or her **Secret Recipe for Success.**

This principle is like a top secret recipe for your favorite dish cooked with common ingredients by a world-renowned chef that you wish you could get your hands on.

The principle is not new; it has been in existence for centuries now. The dilemma most people have is identifying an appropriate role model who would be willing to part with the secret recipe.

Upon identifying your role model, I encourage you to research and study the role model's recipe in full. Stay idealistic and realistic, invest quality time in collecting all data provided by your role model, write it all down step by step in complete detail, and then create your own personalized recipe for success. Become completely obsessed with the recipe because *you become what you think about and act upon*!

Principle #3: Do exactly the same (emulate)—**The Execution Process.**

Execute your planned recipe to achieve your goals. To execute effectively, you must get excited about it. When you are excited about doing something, you will never hesitate to take action. For example, I like to write in order to inspire people, and it excites me to write this book. I sit for hours each day to exercise my mind with ideas on how to make this book as inspirational as possible, utilizing my own personal experiences.

If you are serious about making a difference in your life and the lives of other people, then you must find what makes you excited and take action. The question most people ask me is, "How do you get excited?" Well, the way I get excited is by thinking about the end results, making a difference in people's lives, creating new opportunities, building a legacy, and much more.

These are other popular questions: "How do you formulate an effective plan? What are the critical components?" Consider the following actions:

- Condition your mind.
- Have a plan and plan of action.
- Have effective activity management.
- Identify daily tasks.
- Demand excellence from yourself.
- Prioritize your to do daily and weekly.
- Commit to your work.
- Focus.
- Surround yourself with a positive environment.
- Execute.

We've all had days when we've worked hard and didn't have much to show for it. This happens when you don't have an effective plan and a plan of action. Formulate a clear daily action plan, then weekly, and as you become more effective, you can begin to have a monthly and annual plan. The idea is to learn to utilize your time wisely and effectively in order to produce results.

Knowing how to formulate the plan is half the battle; the other half is knowing how to take action. Until you know the Basic Principles for Success, you won't be able to execute your plan successfully.

At this point in the book, you should have a clear understanding of the three Basic Principles for Success. Prioritize what is important, identify the most critical criteria, and establish numeric goals for them. Label this "Demand Excellence." For instance, if you are in sales, your numeric goals may include how many face-to-face appointments you want to have, how many cold calls you may need to make, and how many sales you want to make. The key is to Demand Excellence in short-term goals.

Depending on your required tasks to achieve your goals, formulate a "*must workweek*", then schedule and arrange your typical prioritized workday—for example, 8:00 AM to 6:00 PM. Focus on taking action one step at the time and one day at the time.

Here are a couple of suggestions:

- What days will you do prospecting?
- What days will you conduct appointments?
- What days will you do administration?
- What days will you get educated?
- What days will you strategize?

Attach those tasks with their appropriate days which coincide with your Demand Excellence.

This "must workweek" must be treated with high level of priority as if it is your sacred bible. Of course, things may change, and flexibility will be required, but commit to sticking to your plan through thick and thin.

Become a *magnet* to the plan. As much as possible, don't alter anything and be sure to stick to it. Some plans may be simple but not easy; be ready to play full out and focus your energy on 10 percent strategy and 90 percent execution because "You become what you think about and *act* upon!"

The Three Basic Principles for Success:

- You must recognize a **Role Model**.
- Ask the role model for his or her **Secret Recipe for Success**.
- Do exactly the same (emulate)—**the execution process**.

Once you have consummated the three Basic Principles for Success, you will have to implement them. The more you use them, the more you will understand them and the more fun you will have with them. However, before you can begin or continue with your career, you must equip yourself with my four fundamentals to success, better identified as "The Principles of Knowing You," in the next chapter.

Master Plan

10% Strategy

And

90% Execution

CHAPTER FIVE

T H E
P R I N C I P L E S
O F
K N O W I N G
Y O U

Chapter Five

If you are going to be successful in creating the life of your dreams, you have to believe that you are capable of making your dreams a reality. You must believe that you have the tools, the knowledge, and the ability to execute the plan of your dreams.

You must believe in yourself. Whether you call it self-assurance, self-esteem, or as I call it, The Principles of Knowing You, the deep foundation of self-belief that you possess is all it takes, along with the conviction and skills to create your most desired results.

Believe in yourself and let no one or anything bring you down; never underestimate what is inside you, for that is what makes you so magnificent. This section of the book is all about you and what makes you so remarkable, demonstrating the true meaning of *Unleash the Magnet in You.*

You must focus and clearly understand the following four principles, which I will clearly outline to provide you with the tools to enhance your present situation and help you travel from where you are today to where you want to go tomorrow. I emphasize that the decisions we make and the actions we take will make all the difference in our lives—as long as we develop winning *I can* attitudes.

Principle #1: Know who you are.

One subject that is overlooked and definitely not studied enough in school is the subject of *you*! However, this subject is essential to your own happiness, quality of life, and overall success. I feel that the most exciting quest you will ever embark on is the journey within yourself.

When you begin to discover the remarkable person you are, you will be able to better understand others, make good career choices and lifestyles, find significance in your life, and earn your own happiness.

Knowing yourself involves seeing yourself objectively and being honest with yourself. Just be yourself; don't fake who you are. Bringing out your own values and beliefs is an essential part of knowing yourself, and that extends deeply into a leader's character.

Consider the following points to formulate who you are:

- What is your personal identification?
- What differentiates you?
- What's your brand?
- What is your compelling story?
- Do you have a unique talent?
- What is your momentum?
- What is your reputation?
- Do you create a presence in your absence?
- What is the magnet in you?
- What's your value proposition?

To do this effectively, you should compose a thirty- to sixty-second biography of yourself, utilizing the points above. Edit it so it represents exactly the way you want people to see you.

Principle #2: Know exactly what you do. *When you are great, the world should know you are great!*

Knowing exactly what you do probably has become second nature to you; nevertheless, people need to know this. Therefore, make certain that you tell people exactly what you do.

As soon as you meet most people, the first thing they want to know is who you are and what you do, but unless you spell out exactly what you do, they won't know what you're great at. This basic information is so overlooked, yet it makes a world of a difference when dealing with people.

Let me give you a personal example. When I was primarily in sales, I found myself attending many social gatherings, which served as a vehicle for prospecting. When I introduced myself to new people, I used to say that I was in the *relationship building* business. That saying piqued a lot of people's attention and therefore got me a lot of appointments, opening doors to market financial services products.

As an entrepreneur, I have a written thirty-second introduction of my companies, and as a speaker, I have short videos and short personal biography that I stick to. Take a look at the points below to formulize your own personal way to know exactly what you do:

- Know your exact job description.
- Know what you do and how you do it.

- Know your deepest level of performance.
- Know your maximum impact.
- Know your personal quest.
- Know your precise behavior.
- Know your precise implementation process.

It is important to know how to introduce yourself effectively and without awkwardness. Avoid blurting out your name, especially when introducing yourself or when leaving a message. We've all heard those messages where people either blurt their names and telephone numbers so fast that you have to listen to them many times to clearly understand them. Don't let this be you!

When in person, get a person's attention first with a simple good morning, good afternoon, or hello to break the ice and make a connection. Look the person in the eyes with a smile and then clearly introduce yourself and explain what you do, using the previous bullet points.

Principle #3: Know precisely what you can provide.

Today's business environment is becoming increasingly complex and competitive due to competition, technology, information, product creation, branding, and scepticism, therefore rendering traditional business solutions obsolete.

For every product or service, there is an overwhelming number of choices to choose from, leaving customers confused and dazed. Therefore, you need to stand out from the rest of your competitors. Remember that providing product, service, and support is just not enough because everyone claims to provide such things.

Be known as a maven in your field and provide world-class service.

The points below are some sample questions you should familiarize yourself with to strategize what precisely you can provide.

- Do you know your value proposition?
- Do you provide the unexpected?
- Do you offer a specialty?
- Do you offer extreme service?
- Are you accountable and transparent?
- Do you walk the talk?
- Are your customer's *wishes* your *command*?

As a motivational speaker, this is how I identify myself: I help people identify a process of behavior on how to unleash the magnet within themselves.

Principle #4: Know why people should deal with you. *People want to deal with the very best! What do you stand for?*

Before people ever do business with you, they must first trust that you are capable of solving problems, and that you are an expert at what you do. A first impression will last a lifetime. Sharing your story and providing people with a clear vision of your strategy and implementation process will definitely get you to the next level of trust.

Don't just ask people for their business; earn the right to their business. Once people begin to like and trust you, they will begin to have the desire to do business with you.

Below I have provided a few points for you to use as a guide in formulizing your own personal way to know why people should deal with *you*.

- Do you have a great reputation?
- Do you have great differentiation?
- Do you provide great client satisfaction?
- Do you have great value proposition?
- Do you have the right strategy?
- Do you reconnect them with their passion?
- Do you add value to their lives?
- Do you have the right fit for their needs?

In summarizing this section of the book, I believe that you are now equipped with the three Basic Principles for Success and The Principles of Knowing You.

Focus all your thinking on the many ways to achieve your goals because when you don't, nobody else will. You must unconditionally believe in yourself at times when no one does. Your strong belief is what will make you a winner and set you apart. However, that's *not* all!

Before you can have any meaningful success in your life or business, you must first develop a winning attitude and the expectation for success. It's all about your attitude and how you think—the decisions you make and the actions you take.

Although all four principles are equally important, the first one— "Know who you are"—is the foundation since you never get a second chance at making a first impression. Per my suggestion earlier, compose a thirty- to sixty-second biography (infomercial) about you and your business. Focus on who you are, know exactly what you do, know precisely what you can provide, and know why people should deal with you. Recite it over and over until you fully memorize the complete infomercial, and then test yourself on how well you will perform when the opportunity presents itself. Will you have resilience?

This exercise can be a little frustrating or even tedious at times for some people because we all believe to know ourselves well. However on the other hand, most people don't know an effective way of presenting themselves to the general public in order to be received exactly the way which we want them to.

I compare this exercise with writing a hit song. When a hit song is written, does the artist change it around every time he or she performs it? The answer is *no*! For the same reason we shouldn't change who we are, exactly what we do, knowing precisely what we can provide, and know why people should deal with us, every time we present ourselves.

Have a canned introduction presentation and stick to it. Modify it only if situations change.

Principle #1: Know who you are.

Principle #2: Know exactly what you do

Principle #3: Know precisely what you can provide

Principle #4: Know why people should deal with you

CHAPTER
SIX

T H E
G U A R A N T E E D
F O R M U L A
F O R   S U C C E S S
BASED ON THREE CRITERIA

Chapter Six

When I talk about *guaranteed*, I must talk about it with discretion because anything guaranteed usually comes with a price tag. However, after paying the price, the reward can be remarkable.

Before you can have any meaningful success in your life and business, you must develop a winning attitude and the expectation for success. This depends solely on the decisions you make and the actions you take.

Make it clear to yourself that the key to a more successful you is based on choosing the right path, and that there is an effective formula for choosing that path. This formula is so effective, and when you meet all three of its principles, your success is absolutely guaranteed!

I've been asked many times, "What is the guaranteed formula for success?" Well, there is not only one way to scale a mountain; there are many ways. Similarly, there is not one path to success, but many. Choose one path, stay on it, and you'll eventually reach your destination. Nevertheless, since I was asked, I'll give my own formula. However, only you can decide whether it's the right path for you.

The principles for The Guaranteed Formula for Success work more effectively when in harmony, but adapting to one or two of the principles may lead you to develop and follow your own path.

Before I give my formula, I'll give you my definition of The Guaranteed Formula for Success. My definition of can be summed up as achieving *your* goals, whatever they may be. This can be narrowed down to the six criteria below:

Decision + Knowledge + Sincere Care + Strong Desire + Implementation + Feelings = Success

Now, following the three main principles, let's take a close look at the six criteria from above, which can guarantee you the formula for success in more detail.

The Three Principles:

- You should have significant knowledge about the business you are in.
- You should sincerely care about the business you are talking about.
- You should have a strong desire to teach your knowledge and feelings to your listeners.

I like to say that applied knowledge is power; therefore, you must have significant knowledge and understanding about who you are and the type of business you're in. Imagine being at a business presentation where your audience knows more about the topic than you do. In this situation, you won't be able to accomplish much unless you're putting a completely new spin on your subject. Significant knowledge is definitely the foundation of everything we do; however, it's meaningless if we don't sincerely care about everything we do.

Even when you may not be having a great day, you must always act with legitimacy and with excitement—and you'll begin to feel legitimate and excited. Act as if you truly care and you'll begin to truly care. Just try it.

I have run into situations where people have had tremendous knowledge and care about their businesses; however, they possessed little to no desire to share their knowledge and feelings with their clients. This can cause them to become completely handicapped in their businesses and possibly in their personal lives as well.

You must influence yourself to acquire the full package. Come to terms with yourself that you are the full package. The confidence generated by significant knowledge of your subject, bolstered by your sincere belief in your topic and the strong desire to share your knowledge and strong feelings, will produce an unbeatable combination.

Once you have met the three principles above, implemented the three Basic Principles for Success, and identified and mastered The Principles of Knowing You, you can then begin to *Unleash the Magnet in You*! Now you will see that being a magnet can allow you to have whatever it is you want just by taking action.

> # Happiness * Health * Wealth

In this section of the book, I will give you a more simplified meaning of each principle as defined below.

Significant knowledge: Having expertise and skills acquired through education and experience; the theoretical or practical understanding of your subject and what is known in a particular field combined.

Acquiring significant knowledge may involve a complex and cognitive process, observation, learning, communication, association, and interpretation. The expression "significant knowledge" can also be used to mean the tremendous confident understanding of a particular subject with the ability to use it for a specific intention when appropriate. When you have significant knowledge, you will be in a position to present yourself to your peers, friends, family, and associates in a position of strength.

Sincere care: To sincerely care without a doubt, you must be an individual who is forthright, truthful, honest, open, straightforward, and unaffected. When you sincerely care about yourself, those around you, the work you do, and the goods you provide, you will start transferring that enthusiasm to others automatically, just for the reason that you sincerely care.

When you meet someone in a social or a personal setting, it's important to let that person know that you sincerely care. This may be done by sending a brief e-mail or a note on a postcard, expressing that you hope the person's experience with you was a meaningful and encouraging one. Mention that you sincerely care about the person's entire family and want to be there to support them.

Sincerely care about you, the people around you, and what you do in your personal life and business. Even though interruptions are a part of life and cannot be avoided sometimes, do your best to give undivided attention and respect to those around you and your task at hand. There are people who depend on you and the work you do. It's important that you put yourself in their shoes and look at the full picture from their perspective.

When you sincerely care, you will realize that you have the potential for excellence, and that excellence will be realized in your daily life and work.

Never think that a particular task is beneath you. Seek to raise the significance of what you're doing by playing full out and giving your absolute best every time. Remember that each effort will be an opportunity for you to express your highest and most treasured values in what you do. Each task is an opportunity for you to transform your vision into reality.

I strongly believe that the greatest and most valuable achievements you can have in life and business are the ones built with a genuine deep, burning passion. When you put passion and care into your daily life, the results can be outstanding.

Strong desire: This is our standard model of human motivation (sometimes this is called the human theory of motivation), requiring that one takes a desire to believe in oneself. You see, belief by itself will not suffice unless the objects of belief interact with your strong desires. Wanting something badly enough is known as strong desire.

If your desire is to make people happy, travel the world, climb Mount Everest, or be successful in your business, then having a strong desire is a huge piece of your puzzle. Therefore, when you have a strong desire so deep that it drives you to achieve your objectives no matter what obstacles you must overcome, the only decision required is taking action. You can get whatever you want if you have a burning passion to accomplish your visions and dreams. We all have the ability to achieve whatever we want.

The forces around you can provide you with what you desire as long as you ask. Therefore, it's important to always think positively and stay motivated about the things you most desire achieving in your life and business.

Teach your knowledge (sharing): When you feel good and have significant knowledge about something or someone, it makes it easy to teach others what you know. There are many ways you can go about this, depending on what you want to accomplish.

When it pertains to business, I will give you a few ideas that you can use effectively. Depending on the type of business you are in, you will need to be cautious and compliant with privacy, copyright, and rules and regulations regarding methods of sharing information.

Some of the most effective ways to teach others are via face-to-face meetings, e-mails, seminars, letters, webinars, videos, and compact discs (CDs). When it comes to sharing your knowledge with everyday people, use the everyday setting and start or join a conversation. This will eventually lead into your topic, given that it is one of interest.

People are always interested in learning about new and interesting topics and ideas that will assist them in enhancing their quality of life. Share with others what you know and teach them how to teach others, and before you know it, a lot of people will know what you know.

Feelings: Our feelings are a natural response to our thoughts and intentions. We don't really choose our feelings directly. Our feelings are a feedback mechanism that we get from being passionate about our lives, our relationships, our careers, and our products and services.

Our feelings indicate whether we're moving into alignment with our true desires' positive or negative feelings. In other words, we humans feel good when we're moving toward the things we want, and we feel terrible when we're moving away from the things we want. This movement is more about our thoughts and our intentions than it is about our actions.

When dealing with feelings, you need to be cautious of good feelings versus bad feelings. Sometimes a bad feeling is a good thing because a bad feeling can always be converted into a good feeling. For every bad feeling, there is an opportunity, and you need to be able to identify it. In this case, you need to share your good feelings with the people you are dealing with either on a personal or professional level. It's important to be your true self and bring out your true feelings.

It's a fact that negative thinkers view a difficulty in every opportunity, and positive thinkers views an opportunity in every difficulty. Be the latter and enjoy an optimistic life!

What Is
"Unleash the Magnet in You ™"?

"Unleash the Magnet in You" is a process of behaviour which will allow you to become completely irresistible and magnetic to everyone you meet and or talk to. It's the process of understanding and making it clear to your mind that LIKE attracts LIKE!

I repeat...LIKE attracts LIKE!

CHAPTER SEVEN

MAGNETIC BEHAVIOUR

Chapter Seven

Magnetic behavior is all about having the power of attracting people to you. Some people seem to naturally attract people to them, while others seem to drive people away. The former make people feel good, while the latter make people feel terrible. If you make people feel good, you'll never be without friends, and if you make people feel terrible, you'll never have friends. Most people are somewhere between these extremes.

I don't feel that magnetizing people comes down to chance; I believe we're in control of who we magnetize into our lives. If you've had trouble magnetizing people that make you feel good into your life, then you will find this section of the book especially interesting. When you magnetize like-minded positive people, together you can focus on obtaining your desires. Positive individuals will always encourage and support your dreams. It's also important for you to understand that negative individuals will have the opposite effect.

In this section of the book, I will show you how you can attract people to you without being a movie star, singer, or any other type of celebrity. I believe that all people can attract others to them by simply being themselves, for the reason that you are the only one who can create your own reality! Let's look at some simple ideas as to how you can begin to possess magnetic behavior.

Idea #1:

You don't need to become a master communicator right from the start. Take small steps and begin to say hello to individuals you've seen before or those who simply look approachable, whether at the mall, supermarket, school, church, the corner store, the elevator, or at your workplace. This will open them up, and the next time you meet, they will be more receptive and inclined to start a conversation with you. In other words, you break the ice.

Idea #2:

Start your day right. When you get out of bed each morning, what kinds of thoughts are running through your mind? Start thinking about putting out only positive vibrations to everyone you meet and talk to. This way, you will begin to attract people who are putting out positive vibrations just like you. Convince yourself that today will be a fantastic day, and that everyone around you will assist in making it so. You need to have a permanent smile on your face throughout the day, especially with your family, co-workers, friends, and new people you meet. This will put you in charge of your thoughts and actions. Even though this can be difficult to control sometimes, by doing this you will have full control and responsibility for the people you magnetize into your life.

Idea #3:

Become a learner and a questioner.

People like to talk about themselves, so a great way to break the ice and create interest in you is to begin by putting others in a comfortable place by listening and asking questions about themselves. Don't overtalk about yourself like an open book. It is okay to state your name and a little about yourself if the individual you are meeting asks, and then you can give a little more. You should always maintain a slight air of mystery, for if you tell them everything about yourself today, they will have no need to meet you tomorrow.

Idea #4:

In contrary to the idea above, you will also need to be careful if you are emitting negative signals to those you know and meet. This may be difficult sometimes; however, you must erase all negative thoughts and behaviors in your life, as this can only lead to magnetizing negative people into your life. People respond to kindness and positivity a lot better than they do to negativity. Odds are, if you are nice to someone (simply saying hello when you meet them), he or she will respond in the same manner. Like attracts like! Demagnetize the negative.

Idea #5:

It has been asked time and time again: What is magnetic behavior? The definition of magnetic behavior is being turned on twenty-four hours a day, seven days a week. It's about understanding that like attracts like, and that people will like you more when you like yourself more.

Idea #6:

Magnetic behavior is doing the things that will bring you joy, happiness, and laughter. Since it has been proven that what you think and what you feel is what will happen in your life, you must understand that events materialize out of thoughts. Whatever it is you want, you can be a magnet to it! You become what you think about and *act* upon!

Idea #7:

When you find yourself in the middle of a positive situation, great! Take action toward making the situation even more positive. Then you will be viewed as an individual of high social importance, and you will become much more attractive to those around you.

You may believe that personal power is a result of chemistry or a social skill that you cannot learn; if so, you are always destined to be someone who does not attract attention. However, you can change all of that by following some simple but effective steps toward improving your self-confidence and image and learning how to engage others more easily.

Idea #8:

Join a networking group (although you don't need to call it that), where you can meet like-minded people who share the same interests as you. Or start your own networking group. Find a unique format that you know would interest people and be beneficial to their behavior of becoming a magnet. Always be original, interesting, and informational. Create an environment where great people can meet and share their interests.

Idea #9:

A good friend of mine has a simple but effective display of magnetic behavior. He has an e-mail signature in red: "If you meet someone without a smile, give them one of yours" (Proverbs). This was so effective on me when I first read it that I immediately picked up the telephone and called him to thank him for putting a smile on my face.

Idea #10:

Mastering the art of communication skills is a fundamental part of your life in which you should invest plenty of time. Communication is the foundation of magnetic behavior, and it is essential for success. The many ways in which you can master your communication skills are by taking courses, reading books, listening to CDs, watching DVDs, and attending workshops and seminars. Naturally, you then need to implement what you learn.

Effective communication is all about conveying your message to other people clearly and unambiguously. It's also about receiving information that others are sending to you, with as little distortion as possible.

Doing this involves effort from both the sender of the message and the receiver of the message. The process can be fraught with error, with messages muddled by the sender or misinterpreted by the recipient, which can cause tremendous confusion, wasted effort, and missed opportunities. In fact, effective communication is only successful when both the sender and the receiver understand the same information as a result of the communication.

Idea #11:

Self-image—What does it mean to you? What does it mean to others around you?

Self image is the way you see yourself. It can be the way you see yourself physically, and it can also be your opinion of whom and what you are, which is normally considered self-perception. It is important, for it affects your self-esteem and confidence in what you think you look like, your personality, the kind of person you believe you are, what you believe others think of you, how much you like yourself or think others like you, and the status you feel you have.

Image is about how you see yourself and how you feel others see you. Remember what I said before and work on this area of your life because the more you like yourself, the more magnetic you'll become to others. But don't become arrogant or haughty.

Idea #12:

Trust

Trust is the foundation of relationship and confidence. A trusted individual is presumed to seek for fulfillment in policies, ethical codes, law, and their previous promises.

In this situation, trust needs to involve belief in the good character, good deeds, or morals of the other party. People engaged in a relationship (whether business related or personal) need to trust each other. Therefore, trust is a strong kind of magnetic behavior. Trust is a prediction of reliance on action, based on what an individual knows about the other individual.

Trust is a statement about what is otherwise unknown (i.e., because it is far away, cannot be verified, or is in the future). For example, most of us trust in God, our friends, our doctors, our parents, and our role models—and when people trust you, you are magnetizing them.

Idea # 13:

Believe

When you believe, you act, and when you act, others believe. Your belief system is the actual set of precepts from which you live your daily life, those which govern your thoughts, words, and actions.

Without these precepts, you could not function. So in order to have magnetic behavior, take this journey, and give it some meaning, you must answer the following questions for yourself:

- Where did you come from? Where are you presently? Where are you going?
- Do you have a strong belief system about yourself, your business, your knowledge, your framework and your execution plan?

Once you have answered the questions, analyzed your answers, and dealt with them, then you will be able to have magnetic self-image and behavior in a position of strength, and people will be attracted to you and whatever you do.

Idea #14:

Branding

Branding doesn't necessarily have to start and end with a logo; in fact, it's a lot more than a logo. Factually, a brand is an idea and perceived value formed by its intended audience, based on an individual's culture, product, and service.

A unique system that includes the logo, style, and color scheme is typically the starting point of a brand. However, it can branch out to exactly how you identify yourself to people you meet and talk to, what types of people you deal with, and what clothes or fragrance you wear. Branding yourself is a fantastic way of utilizing magnetic behavior to attract people to you and your business.

Idea #15:

This idea can be challenging for most people; however, I encourage you to condition your mind to change your conditioning and alter your habitual way of behaving first thing in the morning. Every single morning when you get out of bed, you must program your mind-set and make it a goal to put a smile on your face and on the faces of everyone you meet and talk to. Make them feel that they are special—and that they have done something so special that it will make a positive difference in their lives.

Here is something I learned a couple of years ago from a friend of mine, Mr. George Harrison. Whenever I met with George, I would approach him with a handshake and say, "George, how are you?" He would then respond by saying, "Fantastic, but more importantly, how are you, Don?" I thought this was so special that I quickly started using this form of greeting, and without a doubt, it puts a smile on people's faces 100 percent of the time. Focus on the big prize: the *smile* and the difference you will make.

I've given you fifteen great ideas about how to possess magnetic behavior in you life and business. Once you get the full picture, you can then begin to strategize your own magnetic styles and ideas.

CHAPTER EIGHT

P L A Y   T O
W I N

Chapter Eight

I've always believed that everything that happens in our lives is because of the decisions we make and the actions we take. Moreover, when we take the ultimate challenge, we become what we think about and act upon.

Have you ever been in a situation where you played in a game and your team and the opposition played fantastically? Suppose that it was a game of sales, and everyone sold very well. It was the greatest sales game you ever played in, from the beginning to the end, with everyone performing to the optimum. When the final whistle blew, the winner won by one single sale because the team had made a decision to take focused actions that would only lead to winning, even if it was only by one sale, and they did. They played to win.

Let me ask you a question: Do you always play to win … or do you just play? What does this question mean to you in the context of your own life and business?

This is a fundamental question if you want to achieve your ultimate goals. You must have ultimate goals and dreams. I see people playing it safe every day to avoid losing, rather than playing their hardest to win. If you play to win, it means you're not afraid of rejection, and as a matter of fact, you invite rejection.

When you play to win, you must calculate and be the ultimate risk taker. Prepare yourself and always be ready and willing to go the extra mile. Don't give up with the first sign of resistance caused by rejection or confrontation. Be hungry, never show fear, have a motive to win and always be ready to face your task at hand with confidence.

Never settle! Play to win—push harder, feel the pain, and do not allow the idea of playing it safe to get into your mind—and you will be open to a world of possibilities.

Define your vision, refine your mission, create a strategy, set your goals, implement your plans, and start your processes. Maintain your focus and never quit until you've met your objectives—and may the passion you possess become your reality. I wish you the greatest health, happiness, and prosperity in your future.

Let me share with you some qualities that will assist you in the game of playing to win. The main question is this: Do you love to win at everything you do? And are you ready to educate, learn, and implement, even if it hurts, until you win? If the answer is yes, then you have to do the following:

- Think like a champion.
- Be a hard worker.
- Educate yourself.
- Prepare a sound game plan.
- Study the other team's offense and defense.
- Make the most of all your key players.
- Be resourceful, observant, and extremely enthusiastic.
- Expect to win and play to win.
- Be a winner and make those around you winners.

- Be strong.
- Never quit.
- Make today *your* day … every day.
- Love your true self and love others.
- Be fearless.
- Always play to win.

Play to win or don't play at all. In a seminar, I once asked the audience if they knew who the fastest man in the world was, and almost all the people raised their hands. Then I asked who knew who the second fastest man in the world was, and only two people raised their hands. In the world we live in today, you need to play to win and be the very best at whatever it is that you are doing.

So what is the difference between playing to win and playing to lose? When you play to win, you have thoughts of victory and happiness, and when you play to lose, you have thoughts of fear and defeat. These two thoughts have a tremendous relationship.

Negative thoughts create a feeling of gloom in our bodies; the energy radiated by the positive thoughts is reflected in our actions. Therefore, when you play to win, you play with motivation, and when you play to lose, you play out of desperation. The ultimate result, in both cases, is different.

To play to win, you must love yourself and what you do. Don't just exist, because the results can be tremendously different. Loving what you do and just existing have a direct correlation with being successful or unsuccessful.

I've heard some people say that they just want to play, and if that is your objective, there is nothing wrong with that. However, in the world I live in, I can only encourage you to develop yourself step by step and work hard to achieve those wins, even if they're small winnings.

I like to pay golf, and when I go golfing with my friends, as soon as someone has a bad hit, we say, "We're playing to have fun, right?" While I agree, I will focus and think through every shot because I want to play my best game and win—even if it's to beat my last personal best.

CHAPTER
NINE

F O C U S

Chapter Nine

For some people, focusing can sometimes be like pulling a tooth without anaesthetic. This is because they fear giving up the effortless road, or the comfort zone. Being focused and staying focused can be extremely challenging because most people want to become completely focused the same day they commit to the goal of becoming focused.

If you're not presently focused, becoming focused can be like kicking a bad habit. Like a bad habit, you'll need to begin with small steps one day at the time. Let me share a personal experience with you.

Years ago, I was working as an insurance broker. I felt that I was working long, hard hours but accomplishing little. So I decided to get help from one of my mentors. My mentor got me started on planning my whole day. I executed one task at a time without interruption. By the end of the week, I had accomplished more tasks than I had the entire previous month, just because I was more focused.

Following that exercise, I began to experience more success by being more focused. I acquired total conviction and was in charge of my own life. I began investing all my energy in doing what is uniquely right for me. This led me to focus on doing all the right things right instead of all wrong things right—for example, focusing on solutions instead of problems and focusing on positive results-driven activities.

In my walk of life, daily I hear the saying "Time is money," and of course, I hear it mostly from business owners. Business owners understand how important it is to use time wisely. Now, after saying that, you don't need to be a business owner to want to be focused, use your time effectively, and maximize your full potential. Here are a few effective steps that you should take in order to become more focused and productive:

- Have a daily plan and goal.
- Review the plan at the end of the day.
- Manage your activities.
- Take it one step at a time.
- Make the best possible use of time.
- Be aware of your surroundings.
- Become more specific.
- Be aware of your thinking pattern.
- Have effective tools to work with.
- Keep your thoughts from drifting.
- Don't get complacent.
- Stay away from distractions.
- Handle all your paper once.
- Plan ahead and have time specific goals.
- Keep detailed notes and prioritize.
- Maintain a good database and filing system.
- Constantly educate yourself and put it to practice.
- Always begin your day with the essentials.
- Treat yourself following an accomplishment.
- Be realistic.
- Set up alerts.
- Delegate responsibilities.
- Have a mental program.

- Have a fifteen-minute think time daily.
- Eat healthy and exercise regularly.
- Visualize your future clearly.
- Maintain a balanced mood and normal energy levels.
- Have confidence.
- Have a high level of commitment.
- Surround yourself with positive people.
- Have precise objectives.
- Keep your emotions away from your business decisions.

Even though money cannot buy you more time, you certainly can earn more money when you use your time effectively. When managing your activities more intelligently, you will be able to stay focused on the tasks in front of you.

I can't emphasize enough that when you are focused, you become less stressed and will therefore achieve new breakthroughs in your habits, career, finances, health, relationships, and personal and spiritual development.

When you use your mind power to focus consistently on the things you want, you shall receive it. It's that simple. The problem is that many people focus incorrectly and end up going nowhere or, even worse, receiving something they never wished for.

Focusing is like dreaming. When you start focusing, you start forming beautiful color pictures of the things and results you want—as well as the places you want to go.

Like most people, you've probably experienced dreams of taking a walk on the beach, enjoying a beautiful holiday, having a picnic with your family, or just going for dinner at your favorite restaurant. When people have these kinds of dreams, they have a tendency to make them come true. So why not focus, take control of all your dreams, and make them become a reality?

When you focus deeply, you will increase your level of confidence, deal with your challenges, be more passionate, have a purpose, and possess a deeper burning desire to tackle the ultimate challenge, which is *taking action*.

C O M M I T M E N T S

Chapter Ten

I once heard this saying: "Commitment is the enemy of resistance, for it is the serious promise to press on, to get going, no matter how many times you are knocked down. Get up each time and stick to your commitment."

There is absolutely nothing wrong with setting your goals high. As a matter of fact, because you get out of it what you put in to it, I encourage it—as long as you have a high level of commitment.

The most important single factor in individual success is *commitment*. Commitment ignites action. To commit is to pledge yourself to a certain purpose or line of conduct.

It also means practicing your beliefs consistently. There are two fundamental conditions for commitment. The first is having a sound set of beliefs. The second is faithfully live by those beliefs with your behavior. Possibly the best description of commitment is "persistence with a purpose."

Many successful business people are hailed as visionary leaders. On careful inspection, they are found to be individuals who hold firmly to a simple set of commitments, usually grounded in beliefs such as the following: "the very best product money can buy," "the highest possible customer service," or "extreme client service." It is the strength of these commitments, religiously implemented, that led to their success.

It is extremely important that you make certain commitments to yourself and stick to them through thick and thin. Each and every day, you should practice and apply the following exercise:

I, (your name), would like to win, time and time again, at everything I do! And I, (your name), am prepared to educate, learn, and implement until I win, even if it hurts! I will dedicate my life to positive thinking, and I will never allow negativity into my life and business. I will commit myself to focusing on things that I have and am grateful for, as well as the things that I want, and not the things I don't want. I understand that if I focus on what I want and believe, I can achieve it, and then I shall receive it! I believe that I am the best at what I do, and I will make a commitment to myself to let the whole world know about it.

Don't ever underestimate the power of commitment, for it unlocks the doors of our imaginations, allows vision, and provides us with the tools to turn dreams into reality.

Be sure to stay fully committed to yourself. In the past, I have found that some people can stay committed for one week or a month, and others can stay committed for two to three months. However, a true winner will stay fully committed for as long as it takes to win.

When you have desire, you have the key to motivation. When you have determination and commitment to an unrelenting pursuit of your goals and dreams, commitment to excellence will enable you to achieve the level of success you seek and deserve.

I can't stress enough that unless there is full commitment, there are only promises and hopes. Imagine hanging on to promises and hopes. In the early years of my career in financial services, I used to print twelve commitment certificates, fill it out as a sign of pledge and commitment to myself and my company each and every month.

Now, mind you, if you're having trouble making big or long-term commitments, I encourage you to start making small and short-term commitments until you are prepared to take the big plunge. Then, once you are ready to take the plunge in making full commitments, ensure that for the rest of your life you will turn *no, no, no* into *yes, yes, yes*! I commit!

There are many things you can commit to, such as getting in shape, saving for retirement or a new car, learning how to play guitar, or even training to run a marathon. However, the most important commitment you can make is committing to yourself to *take action* on your commitments.

I, *(Your name)*

_____

commit to all the above commitments and I promise to read them daily and live by them to the fullest in my life and business.

CHAPTER ELEVEN

M A G N E T I Z I N G -
M A T E R I A L I Z I N G

Chapter Eleven

I consider magnetizing another human being the single greatest skill we can possess. However, I have also realized that it can be difficult for most people, simply due to their low level of confidence. When magnetizing someone, you should always be affirmative. Your behavior and attitude should be sound in order to create a center of attention for the individual you are magnetizing.

Magnetizing is another word for attracting someone to you. It's all about how you condition your mind and the actions you take. The greatest gift we can have is the capability to magnetize everyone we meet and talk to in our lives and business. This does not have to be a dream; it can be a reality if only we can truly believe, imagine, and take action.

Can you imagine living in a world where everything you dream about can come true—and you can live it to the maximum? Can you imagine living in a world where you can help others realize their own dreams?

Can you visualize living in a world where everything you want you can magnetize to you? Can you envision that just by thinking *happy* thoughts, you will begin to feel *happy* and have the ability to change the environment around you just by changing the way you speak and think? We're all working with one single power, and that is the power of magnetizing—materializing.

By reading and rehearsing the contents of this book, you are invited to take a seat in the driver's seat. You will be able to use your desires and talents to take full control of your destiny. You will define and accept who you are today and who you want to be. You will identify the role players in your life and business. You will be motivated to shake off mediocrity and live up to greatness.

Once you understand and have accepted who you are and what you stand for, then the people around you will accept you for who you are. Then you will form an enviable network of friends and professionals to assist in making all your dreams come true.

Be focused and confident; believe that you have the skills and knowledge necessary to set your wonderful dreams in motion. Surround yourself with like-minded people who will assist you in magnetizing others to you in order to materialize all the wonderful things this universe has to offer.

In order to attract positive magnetism to your life, you must discover a way to turn on your good mood and feelings every single moment you are awake. Taking control of your thoughts and feelings may require a few actions, however.

For example, when I'm feeling a little down, I'll go to the gym, play my favourite song, call a good friend, read a good book, go for a drive in the country, or take my family out for a meal at our favourite restaurant. By doing this, I begin to feel good again and move toward greatness, automatically magnetizing others to my life. Your mind and behavior are in charge of who and what you magnetize to your life.

Have you ever greeted someone with, "How are you?" and their response was, "Not bad"? Well, the response "Not bad" is one of the most negative ways to feel because not bad is obviously not good. When your response is good, then you will feel good and make the people around you feel good. When you feel bad, you will make the people around you feel bad; either you're good or you're bad.

Place yourself in that feel-good place no matter what. Don't let anything or anyone pull you out of that place. Dream and make that place your personal space, only bringing like-minded people to your place of feeling good.

One of the most significant examples I can give you on magnetizing and materializing is one from my own personal life. For years, every time I went out, either alone or with someone else, I used to take a route that was not the fastest when coming home. People used to ask me, "Why are you taking the long way home?" My answer was that I was driving through the neighborhood where my family and I were going to buy our dream home one day. It only took the next seven years before we bought our dream home and moved into that neighborhood.

Life is phenomenal. Take a journey and live your life to the fullest. Learn how to magnetize what you want to materialize in your life. Create your own destiny and don't let anyone or anything stand in your way. No one else can do it for you. You can do it if you just believe enough in yourself, and then others will believe in you. When you're in control of your thoughts and feelings, you can shape your destiny … Your actions today will determine your outcome tomorrow!

It doesn't matter where you are in life right now. To get what you want, you must make a personal commitment to only magnetize those things and people that will assist you in taking action and materializing all you want out of life. Life was meant to be abundant in every way as long as you don't live selfishly.

Live your life with passion and build a legacy.

CHAPTER
TWELVE

S E L F   I M A G E
&
S E L F   E S T E E M
C O N C E P T

Chapter Twelve

As mentioned earlier, self-image is the way you see yourself. This can be the way you see yourself physically, and it can also be your opinion of who and what you are. This is important because it affects your self-esteem and your level of confidence. The better your self-image is, the higher your self-esteem. For example, as a man, when I feel good physically, get a haircut, wear a new suit with matching shirt, tie, belt, shoes, and cufflinks, my self-esteem is way up, and I feel more confident.

A poor opinion of your physical self can cause you to have low self-esteem and lack of self-confidence. In most cases, men worry about how tall they are, how strong they are, how much hair they have, how much they weigh, and how handsome they are. The most horrible thing for men is probably being short and overweight. They believe in the tall, dark, and handsome myth. Some men may also suffer low self-esteem if they think they are short or too skinny. In some cases, these men can become self-image obsessed easily.

Based on my research, self-esteem in people these days seems dependent on how they believe they look. Many people step on the scale several times a day to check their weight. Some may perceive themselves as overweight, short, or skinny, and this may not even be true.

I personally know individuals who are overweight and happy and others who are slim and unhappy. What is important is that you maintain a positive, healthy self-image that allows you to portray yourself in a positive and confident manner. You can decide to be happy with yourself right now and accept yourself, with or without faults.

Most people don't realize it, but the source of many social, physical, and emotional troubles is simply the fact that some people dislike themselves. They don't overall feel good about the way they look, how they behave and even how they talk. People lacking self-image and self-esteem find themselves comparing themselves with others, wishing they were something or someone different. They waste a lot of time thinking, *What if I looked this way or that way? What if I had this or that? What if I had more of this or more of that?*

The secret of unleashing the magnet in you is accepting who you are right now. Quit wishing you were something or someone different. Accept yourself. If God wanted to make you look like a runway model or be an actor, an athlete, or anyone else for that matter, he would have done so.

You don't need to be someone or something else; just work with what you have and become the very best you. Let's look at self-image and self-esteem.

Self-image includes the following:

- What you believe you look like
- The way you see your personality
- What kind of individual you think you are
- What you believe others think of you

- How much you like yourself
- How much you think others like you
- The social status you feel you have

Self-esteem is how you feel about yourself. Self-image is about how you see yourself and how you believe others see you. The two are closely connected in that if you have a negative opinion of yourself, your self-esteem will be negative and suffer. Let's look at twenty-five great steps you can take to begin fostering a positive image of yourself.

1. Take a self-image inventory.
2. Clearly define your personal goals and objectives.
3. Have realistic and measurable goals.
4. Possess a positive mental attitude.
5. Don't compare yourself to others.
6. Develop your unique strengths.
7. Learn to love yourself more.
8. Remember that you are one of a kind.
9. Give positive affirmations.
10. Laugh and smile more.
11. Be aware of your personal growth.
12. Always present yourself the way you want to be perceived.
13. Look your best.
14. Treat others the way you want to be treated.
15. Possess the Magnetism Effect.
16. Have your own faith and belief.
17. Improve your speaking skills.
18. Create new experiences for yourself.
19. Change your mental image.
20. Surround yourself with positive people.
21. Exercise and take care of your body—you are what you eat

22. Take good care of your mind.
23. Help and encourage others.
24. Give and you shall receive.
25. Possess a high level of confidence.

When unleashing the magnet within yourself, it is important that you be nice to yourself. Don't give yourself a hard time. Start appreciating the fact that you are a unique individual. Always celebrate the greatness within you. Highlight every success. How did you do it? What steps did you take? What did it take to succeed? How did you feel about yourself, and what you learned from that experience?

When we think about self-esteem and self-image, we must have dreams; we must visualize how we would like our lives to be. We must set goals for ourselves and compose a realistic plan and a plan of action. We must also have a plan as to what the rewards of our success will be, celebrating all our accomplishments.

Keep a journal of yourself and your actions. I like to make a list of all my accomplishments, and you can do the same. It doesn't matter how big or small. Think of times when you did something rewarding like closing a hard deal, passing an exam, working hard and succeeding at a school project, losing weight, or even helping a good friend. Be proud of your accomplishments and read your list repeatedly.

If you want to boost your self-esteem and self-image even more, do more of the things you love doing, like joining a team, taking music lessons, volunteering, or joining some sort of networking group.

Remember, we are all humans, and humans will make mistakes. Mistakes are a great opportunity to learn more about ourselves.

Accept compliments when given by others because you are worthy of compliments.

Most of all, believe in yourself and trust in your skills and your talents, always remembering that you are in full control of your level of self-esteem and self-image.

Decide today that you will take all the actions necessary to ensure that your self-esteem and self-image gauge always remains on full.

"You become what you think about and act upon"

What do you see when you look in the mirror?

SUCCESS - BE THE MASTER OF YOUR DESTINY

Chapter Thirteen

Our success is determined by our thoughts and expectations, which exercise tremendous power and influence in our lives. I have heard many people say that success is a lifestyle. In life, we don't always get what we want or deserve; however, we generally get a little more than what we expect. In most cases, we receive what we believe. Unfortunately, this principle functions in the positive as it does in the negative. When we believe and take actions towards positive, we will receive positive and when we believe and take actions towards negative, we will receive negative.

The magic question is, what is success? For some individuals, success is being well known and happily married with a couple of children and having a big house with a white picket fence, several cars, a great business, a successful career, money, and investments. What's your definition of success? The meaning of success comes in many forms and many definitions.

The fact is that if you want to be successful, you must focus on following your dreams. Your dreams are the foundation of your success. Your life will follow your dreams, and what you expect and take action on is what you will receive.

It all depends on what you're searching for in your life and business. A musician may have one definition of success, and an insurance broker may have another. An author may see success as having a book hit number one on the *New York Times* best-seller list, and a financial advisor may see success as having many high-net-worth clients and millions of dollars under management. It truly depends on your goals and dreams. Some believe that success is realized when you think and feel successful.

However, it is important that you understand your own true meaning of success. Rather than trying to create my own definition of success, I took a survey and asked a number people to give their individual meanings of success, which I will share with you in a moment.

I believe that there is a distinction between accomplishment, success, and true success. Let's explore this briefly.

Accomplishment is when you have attempted a task or action and obtained the preferred results. This is based on what you expected, and what results were achieved. This is a daily happening in the world and in the marketplace. People sometimes accomplish things all day long but achieve little success in their actions.

Success can be something different. To most people, success is having an ongoing string of accomplishments that, when you put them together, add up to a major obtainment in life. The addition of all the accomplishments in a person's business or life can be viewed as success in his life and business.

Success can be summed up as an ongoing realization and obtainment of worthy desired results, concerning actions, life, business, wealth, or a worthy idea, to say the least.

Some have said that there is an even a higher level of success, and that there is a more powerful level of high achievement—for example, being successful in a marriage, as a parent, as a community worker, as a sibling, and as a friend. This is why we say that success breeds success.

Nevertheless, anyone who has achieved success in any form knows that it is a result of continual concentration based on the level of commitments and actions we take.

As I mentioned earlier, in order to get an array of definitions of success, I contacted many individuals whom I know and believe have reached a certain level of success in their personal lives, businesses, or both. I asked them to share their personal definitions of success. I offered to publish their writing and give them credit, and while most wanted to share their definitions of success, strangely enough, most were too shy to have their names printed in a book.

Everyone is entitled to an opinion, and each person deserves to be respected for it. Whether we believe their opinions are right or wrong, they are right for them. We will begin with the first definition of success, by my good friend, author, speaker, and entrepreneur from British Columbia, Canada, Mr. Simon Reilly.

My definition of success is the experience of living my values, vision, business plan, and ninety-day goals. *Simon Reilly*

- In my own definition, success is setting out a weight loss plan and sticking to the plan until you lose all the weight you set out to lose in the planned timeframe. *Agnaldo Lopes*

- I believe success is attaining certain goals in my life. Money is one of them, but there is more to success than just the monetary aspect of it. I measure success in various ways—for example, the level of comfort I seek, happiness, and most important of all, my health. When I am able to attain the above, I consider myself very successful. *Anonymous*

- For me, success means all of the following: enjoying good health and having a healthy and happy family, great relationships, financial freedom, a great career, and a fulfilling and meaningful spiritual life. *CK*

- Success is doing what I enjoy and being well compensated for it. *Anonymous*

- I see success as achieving what you want the most; this can be passing the examination, owning the car you want or building your dream house, etc. *PB*

- Success is measured by what you have achieved in your life. *Anonymous*

- I consider success to be when you are content with what you have or what you do in life. If you have no complaints about how you live your life, no worries about today, tomorrow, or the day after, then you are successful. *Anonymous*

- I see success as when an individual or organization has attained their goals and objectives. *Anonymous*

- To me, success means achieving the objectives I set for myself. It can be anything from waking up early in the morning to having a good lifestyle, like having a nice home, great friends, being healthy, etc. When I have achieved my objectives, I consider myself successful. *Anonymous*

- I believe that success means the various challenges that I have encountered and managed to overcome. In my view, success is measured by the many battles that one fights and, in the end, overcomes. Then and only then do I consider myself successful. *NB*

- Success means achieving my goals in life and when my goals are fulfilled in my life according to my expectations, and then it means I am successful. *Anonymous*

- I view success as being how good your relationship is with God. The reason is simple: because God is the originator of everything good. Hence, being intimate with God is the most successful thing there can be. *Anonymous*

- To me, success simply means being content. I know of individuals who have all the material things they ever dreamed of having but are extremely unhappy, and I also know of people who have what most people would call "nothing" but are happy. *Anonymous*

- I believe that God created me with a planned life, and as far as I'm concerned, as long as I have a great relationship with God, my family, and my friends, and I'm healthy, then I'm very successful. I don't measure success in monetary terms. *Anonymous*

- Success means *me*—to become the very best me that I can be. To be a unique person without comparing myself to someone else, and to have a great personality, abilities, and talents so that there is no comparison. *Anonymous*

- I define success as the point when your expectations in life are fulfilled, in the areas of both spiritual and material aspects. So to be successful, you need to have a balance in all the key areas of your life. *JC*

- I see success as being successful enough to the point that you can assist others in becoming successful. *Anonymous*

- To me, success is making positive, lasting changes in my life and having real joy, health, happiness, and wealth. And all this comes about when we see that the people we love, like God, family, and friends, are happy. *Anonymous*

- Defining success is not an easy thing; however, I'd say that being successful is enjoying life in everything you do. It is to laugh more, to respect more, accept yourself and others, to manifest, to make a difference for the better, to appreciate the simple things in life, such as beauty, air, nature, etc., and to achieve one's goals. *LD*

- To succeed is to live your life to the fullest and build a legacy— to live a life that you can look back at and have no regrets at all and would want to relive that life all over again. *DLX*

- Success is developing my personal growth in the areas of finance, emotion, physical, mentally, and most importantly, being in a genuine and personal relationship with God. *Anonymous*

- Success means having control of my destiny. Success is here when I have reached the highest level of my life by having all or most of the things that I require to live, having access to them whenever I want. *Anonymous*

- At this stage of my life, this is simple. To me, success means the day that I'll be in a position to take care of my large family without feeling any financial stress. I will also say that being strong spiritually and having a special relationship with God will specially count as a success. *Anonymous*

- I imagine that when one is considered successful, he or she has a strong financial base. Unfortunately, the people who are called successful people in this world are measured mostly by their wealth. In my definition of success, we should also take into consideration good health, happy family life, good employment, good friends, and being spiritually strong. *Anonymous*

- I think true success is having peace of mind, being healthy, being spiritually stable, being able to pay your bills, being debt free, saving your money, loving people and having them love you back. *Anonymous*

- My definition of success means being a goal-setting fanatic, helping people, and thinking and doing everything it takes to win. *Anonymous*

- I envision success as achieving my desired goal and being financially fit, spiritually at peace, and emotional and physically fit. *Anonymous*

- In short, success means living my highest aspirations and my highest ambitions. Living all my dreams along with a fulfilled life, great friends, loving family, good finances, and a great relationship with the good shepherd. *Anonymous*

- I measure success simply as having a nice home for my family, food on the table, a good job or career, a green and beautiful backyard garden for BBQ, good health, and beautiful friends. I also see success as being able to help the sick, the hungry, and the hopeless as well being an inspiration in my community. *SM*

- I envision success as being about developing oneself into an individual who is valuable to others. To be in harmony with your goals, act on your dreams, and eventually be the kind of person who people will respect. *Anonymous*

- I feel that success has arrived in my life when I have good health, financial stability, a good relationship with God, a happy family, own a home, own a nice car, put food on the table, take occasional family vacations, and help others in need. *AL*

There are thirty-two different people and thirty-two similar yet different opinions and definitions of success. One thing's for sure: as I read and typed all of the many definitions and opinions, I concluded that they all have things in common. They were all drenched with emotions, powered by passion, and driven by destiny and a deep, burning desire for success.

When there is passion and desire connected to the heart, true success in any definition is destined to happen eventually. So it is safe to say that success and heart have a definite connection. Over the years, I have met with many successful athletes, singers, musicians, actors, artists, and entrepreneurs, and I have learned that they possess a direct link from their hearts to their individual successes. Is your success linked to your heart?

What is success? Well, that is up to you. As described in many of the above descriptions, it's definitely not only accomplishments. It's much more than that.

I suggest focusing on a steady realization of your dreams and ideas that are driven by your heart and passion, which will guarantee you a lifelong string of success. Set your heart on experiencing a deeper and higher level of success. Success is a journey, not a destination. The future will take care of you if you take care of the present.

Beyond what we consider success and being successful, there are those who have gone where no others have gone before, and I call them the Super Successful. So what do the Super Successful know and do that others don't know and don't do? The Super Successful understand how to apply the Magnetism Effect, and they know how to differentiate themselves! The following traits tend to apply to them:

- Are entrepreneurs
- Are goal-setting fanatics
- Have plan and plans of action
- Are focused
- Have principles and philosophy
- Have a high level of integrity
- Create their own luck
- Are people who know how to dream—and dream big

- Always ask for what they want
- Believe that what they want is already theirs and receive exactly that
- Replace fear with education
- Have passion
- Are visionaries
- Always choose to win
- Lead by example
- Take control
- Are emotionally fit
- Know what they want
- Know how to apply themselves
- Have positive self-images
- Live their best lives now
- Understand that life was meant to be abundant in all areas
- Understand how to build a business instead of getting a "job"
- Know their strengths and leverage them to become successful entrepreneurs
- Live by the saying "Change the way you think and change the way you live!"

Unleash the Magnet in You is about the mind and the behavior. If your life and business are on the right track, I say go full force ahead. If not, then you *must* alter your conditioning and change your habitual way of thinking!

If you didn't understand the last paragraph, read it again and again until you clearly understand the message I want to get across to you. I am sure you have heard the saying "Misery loves company". My own saying is, if you're dragging a heavy bag of misery behind you, drop it off today and move ahead to a more successful you."

This section of the book was packed with great information and ideas to assist you. However, true success can only come from the decisions you make and the actions you take.

You always have two choices: one, you can make excuses; or two, you can be successful. But you can't have both. You choose!

CHAPTER
FOURTEEN

HIGHLY
EFFECTIVE
MAINTENANCE
PRINCIPLES

Chapter Fourteen

As I mentioned previously, this book has been organized and simplified into sections in order to assist you in learning how to unleash the magnet within you to take your life and business to the next level of success. This section will focus on the principles of highly effective maintenance of your business and life.

As a motivator, I also need to be motivated and educated. I attend motivational seminars; read books, newspapers, and magazines; listen to CDs in my car; watch videos; and meet with my mentors on a regular basis. It's extremely important that I keep myself sharp and updated with news around the world in order to stay one step ahead of my competitors.

Things in life never stand still and neither should you. Don't ever count on things getting better—count on making yourself better. There is always a window of opportunity, and the individual who can take the first leap through will win.

In these challenging times, you need to prepare yourself to unleash the magnet within you in order to survive. So in order to be successful, what should you do to prepare? How can you help the people around you do what you do? How can you ensure your own peace of mind? How can you do your best work and achieve your best results ever?

Whose recipe can you use to attract success? These are the types of questions I've asked myself.

Here is my top five list of effective actions to prosper in dreadful times:

1. Have an effective plan and an effective plan of action. Using The Principles of Knowing You, know exactly what you want to achieve in a particular time frame. Write it down, let it happen in your mind, *act* on it, and it will happen in your life.

2. If you're in sales, make prospecting your number one priority. Contact as many people as possible and focus only on results. Treat people as if they are already your clients. Build trust and establish credibility and accountability.

3. Ask for introductions and educate clients on how they should introduce their family members, associates, and qualified friends to you.

4. Revise your value proposition and identify the key players in your business and life, focusing on making those relationships stronger. By key players, I mean your existing clients, your family, your friends, your colleagues, your association, your board of directors, and your networking group. Reiterate what you do, how you do it, and how they can assist you. Create a presence in your absence.

5. Invest quality time researching and understanding the secret of the Super Successful. I understand what it is that the Super Successful know and do, which others don't know and don't do.

You see, the Super Successful understand how to apply the Magnetism Effect, and they know how to differentiate themselves! The Super Successful are entrepreneurs; they are goal-setting fanatics; they have a plan and a plan of action; they are focused; they have principles and philosophies; they have integrity; they create their own luck; and most of all, they live by the saying "Change the way you think and change the way you live!"

In addition to clearly understanding the above and following it in order to be highly effective, you must also have self-awareness and the ability to self-motivate on demand. Be proactive, using your resources and initiative to discover solutions rather than focusing on the problems. Focus 10 percent of your efforts on identifying and understanding the problem and 90 percent of your efforts on identifying the solution and execution.

Remember that you become what you think about and *act* upon. Always put first things first, maintain a positive mental attitude, and seek to understand and be understood. Be a team player and educate yourself. Be able-bodied and educated physically, mentally, spiritually, socially, and emotionally. The key is to maintain an even balance among these dimensions.

One of the most treasured traits you can possess is the trait of listening. God gave us one mouth and two ears for a reason: to listen twice as much as we talk. Effective listening is not simply repeating what the other person has said through the lens of one's own experience. It is putting yourself in the perspective of the other person, listening and understanding for both meaning and feeling.

One of the ways you can assure that you have and maintain highly effective maintenance principles is by developing a personal mission statement. Focus on the things you want to accomplish, what you want to be, and on your values and principles. Each person is unique; a personal mission statement will reflect that uniqueness, both in content and in structure.

Remember, it's all about the decisions we make and the actions we take. Rapidly learn about the changes that are reshaping your industry, your life, and master them.

In my case, I'm pursuing supremacy in the areas of being an author, speaker, a business owner, a great family man, a humanitarian, and a good son to God. I live life full of passion, using assistance from my mentors and board of directors. Life was meant to be abundant in all areas. Live your life with passion and build a legacy.

To have highly effective maintenance principles, you will need to possess a high level of passion, discipline and follow certain proven principles in order to go from where you are presently to where you want to go in the future. Stay focused on your strengths and get rid of everything that is holding you back from achieving your success.

CHAPTER
FIFTEEN

S E L F
M A N A G E M E N T
P R I N C I P L E S

Chapter Fifteen

Self-management and self-objectives must go hand in hand. Without a doubt, when we think about self-management, we first must think about our objectives. Our objectives should be about what we want to achieve. Objectives are what we must have in order to take effective action. It's the ultimate reason to enter serious business conversation or undertake any form of communication in which you have a point to make.

The way I see it, having the ability to manage your personal reaction to responsibilities and challenges in life and business is called self-management. This can involve managing your activities and adapting to changing situations. It requires you to reflect on your experiences and their effects on your physical and mental state. Self-management requires the background skills and experiences that you have learned and adapted to. Many effective steps go into learning and mastering a solid self-management principle. In this section of the book, we will explore the many different steps that are crucial in effective self-management and unleashing the magnet within you.

SELF-LEARNING

In the world we live in, if you are amongst one of the fortunate individuals, you will study approximately 25 percent of your life, yet that is still not enough to learn everything you need to know. Self-learning is about having the ability to recognize gaps in your knowledge and obtain it independently.

You will need to have the power and desire to continue to learn beyond the structured knowledge provided by your school and what you have gained in work experience. I personally know a lot about this because after high school, I didn't have the opportunity to attend college right away. All the college courses I later took identified the gaps in my knowledge. Furthering your learning requires innovation, drive, initiative, and a framework. Self-learning requires self-motivation and knowledge of your personal learning styles and preferences. The bottom line is, you'll never know enough; life is an endless learning process. Find your personal style and preference and just do it.

OBJECTIVE SKILLS

Objective skills are exciting. They are about having the necessary ability to create, plan, and achieve amazing personal and professional goals. Knowing what is important to you allows you to direct your attention and effort toward those things, by setting long-term and short-term goals. Objective skills require you to have the ability to set specific time frame goals that are acceptable to you, realistic, and have definable results. To achieve your goals requires persistence, motivation, goal orientation, and the drive to execute in order to succeed.

PERSONAL AWARENESS

Personal awareness is the observation of your skills, capability, knowledge, values, and responsibilities, both professionally and personally. This can be difficult for most people; therefore, get an honest opinion from someone you respect and trust. It's about being capable of recognizing your raw talents, having self-confidence, and knowing what you can carry out. Of course, this includes having the ability to boldly improve on and expand new talents and skills.

VERSATILITY

When we speak about versatility, the first thing that comes to mind is someone having a wide variety of skills and having the ability to adapt to new situations and the application of those skills. It also includes possessing the ability to acquire new skills learned from educators, role models, or mentors in your particular field. This all means that you must be fully committed to working with individuals with many different levels of understanding, values, views, and backgrounds. To have versatility is to have flexibility and expandability.

ACTIVITY MANAGEMENT

There are only twenty-four hours in a day. For as long as I can remember, I've been hearing about time management. I'm still not convinced that we can actually manage time. The way that I understand time management is recognizing the many different demands in your twenty-four hours, setting priorities, and scheduling your activities according to your goals, responsibilities, and needs. This also includes the need for food, relaxation, and social and spiritual life.

To be effective, I personally use a day planner and a contact management system to schedule and manage all my obligations and keep track of my appointments and commitments. With all the new technology today, we have more effective ways of taking control of our twenty-four hours in order to maximize effectiveness and minimize stress. The use of iPhones, BlackBerrys, Microsoft Office Outlook, and many other activity management programs can be helpful. The twenty-four hours per day that we are given can individually be wisely organized based on your own priorities and objectives.

COMMITMENT

When I look at commitment and what it means, I envision various definitions and insight. In this case, we must look at self-commitment and commitment to those around us whose lives we impact, and vice-versa. To me, commitment is like making a pledge to yourself, your family, your job, your spouse, your children, the people who trust and depend on you, and God.

It's about being dependable and trustworthy, the willingness to commit, possessing a high level of determination to achieve success, and focusing on the target of your commitments. Commitment ignites actions; therefore, commitment is an extremely significant factor in your success.

There are two essential conditions for commitment. One is having strong beliefs, and the second is having faithful devotion to those beliefs. Be wise and live by the old saying "Stand for something or you'll fall for anything." Make a commitment to yourself and stick to it through thick and thin. When your level of commitment is strong and followed devotedly, this will lead you straight to success.

GOAL SETTING

Effective goal setting plays a major role in establishing specific, measurable, and time-targeted objectives because goal setting is a major component of personal development.

In goal setting, the more motivated you are, the higher you will set your bar. The less motivated you are, the lower you will set your bar. In setting goals, you will have the opportunity to examine your desires, interests, responsibilities, and commitments, identifying goals that are important to you and making a commitment to working hard toward achieving your goals.

It is important that you set realistic, clearly defined goals with a specific time frame. This way, progress can be measured and success judged clearly. For example, "I will be skinny" is not a good goal because it is unclear. However, "I want to set an effective weight loss exercise routine four times per week, ninety minutes per day" is a better and workable goal.

Have a tracking system of your progress; you may adjust or even add to it. This is a fantastic way of continually monitoring development in your life and business. Setting goals can serve as an energizer, which will affect persistence and activate cognitive knowledge and strategies to assist you with all the situations at hand. The fuel for continuous setting and execution of your goals is the satisfaction in accomplishing positive results, even if they are small.

PLANNING AND EXECUTING

In my own words, planning means to strategize, and executing means to act upon. I normally allocate 10 percent of my time to planning and 90 percent to executing my plan. In planning, you need to develop a detailed, realistic framework to solve a problem or to reach a certain goal. The plan needs to be reviewed regularly to accommodate any changes in your situation and priorities. Continually monitor the success of your strategy in order to reach your original goal within the set time frame.

Coming up with a plan can be easy. However, the execution process can sometimes be challenging, and without a successful execution plan, your strategy will fail. When you are good at executing your plan, the first thing you need to do is establish an implementation plan. Focus and prioritize your actions, assigning responsibilities if working with a group. Address resources needed, identify tools of communication, measure your progress, and present an opportunity to celebrate success.

If you lack motivation to execute, I suggest that you follow the action plan above at a much slower pace by taking smaller execution steps. For example, in sales, prospecting is your number one activity. Instead of going out to see potential clients all day long, make a plan to start prospecting for three or four hours per day, and when you get good at it, then go for a full day.

SELF-APPRAISAL

I believe in working hard and playing hard. Self-appraisal is an essential part of the performance appraisal process, wherein you give feedback regarding your performance. Usually this is done with a standard self-appraisal form, and you rate yourself on various parameters. By doing this you will objectively analyze your own situation, your skills, and your qualities, recognize your strengths and weaknesses, and acknowledge areas of improvement so that you can identify areas to improve on. An effective self-appraisal is strongly recommended so you can remove or minimize any roadblocks that may interrupt your success.

When completing the appraisal form, always be honest in listing your accomplishments and failures. Don't overstate your strengths and don't hide your weaknesses. A self-appraisal is also known as the self-assessment quiz. Be prepared with all the evidence necessary, be objective, bring a positive attitude, cover all aspects, and look for future responsibilities. If you are not comfortable monitoring the self-appraisal process yourself for any reason, then ask someone you trust to carry it forward for you.

Are you in a supportive environment, where the people around you will motivate you toward success? Or are you in an environment where people will hold or pull you backward? Answer these questions and decide if you need to make changes in your current environment.

You are the only person who can correctly answer these questions, and you're the only person who can change your life. One thing is for sure: I want you to learn how to unleash the magnet within you and be very successful.

In the self-management principles section of this book, we will go more in depth as to how to enable yourself to manifest new knowledge and understanding through the process of developing your personal skills and therefore simplifying the understanding of how to unleash the magnet within you.

"Know and understand yourself first so others
can know and understand you"

Sample Self-Appraisal

To be completed and submitted to your manager prior to performance review and career development discussion.

Name:
Position:
Manager:
Date:

Overall Performance Strengths and Development Required

1. **Performance strengths.** Indicate your three major strengths and provide one example or accomplishment for each:
   a)
   b)
   c)

2. **Development required.** Indicate the three most important things you want to accomplish, improve, and/or eliminate in order to maximize your potential, and the steps you plan to take to address them.

   Areas for development   Action steps to assist development
   a)
   b)
   c)

3. In your opinion, what roles, responsibilities, and/or duties that you perform are the most value added to this company?

4. **How can your position provide even more value to this company** (i.e., what activities, processes, reports, and tools would you develop and implement to provide better information, support, assistance, etc.)?

5. **Career goals.** In terms of your career and professional development, what roles or responsibilities would you like to take on to expand your skills and knowledge?

6. **Additional discussion**. Are there any other topics or issues you would like to discuss with your manager?

INFLUENCE
YOURSELF BY
INFLUENCING
OTHERS

Chapter Sixteen

Your actions today will determine your outcome tomorrow, and you can influence others to dream and take action to become the best they can be, making you an excellent influencer and leader.

As always, I encourage you to read this book as often as you can in order to get the full effect. Highlight the topics that are more significant to you in your life and business. You will discover that with each read, you will not only reinforce what you already know, but you will also rediscover new information that may not have registered the first time. In my experience, I have found that it takes time to absorb and assimilate all of the ideas when reading a book once.

I encourage you to give this book to family members, friends, and associates. This will allow them to begin thinking the way you do, thereby making it easier to communicate and eventually make amazing changes in their lives and businesses. The greatest gift you can give someone is the gift of super empowerment, love, and understanding. This process may be considered the simplest and most effective way of influencing yourself and others.

We were all born with the power to create and develop the lives we want, the lives we dream about, and the lives meant for us to live. We must earn this through hard work, which naturally involves learning, focusing, applying, and living by the time-tested, ageless process and guaranteed principles. I learned these principles from individual study, school, work, church, and by following successful people and acting on their successful recipes. I clearly understood that these principles have been passed down from generation to generation by mentors, teachers, coaches, books, seminars, workshops, videos, and audio programs.

This book reveals the principles that will help you possess the Magnetism Effect and unleash the magnet within you to attract positive people to you in your life and business.

Why should you spread the word and influence others? It's simple. If you're a leader and an influencer, then you must think about what it would mean if you could influence all your family, friends, and associates to get rid of the negative and replace it with positive. What if you could influence all your family, friends, and associates to turn *no, no, no* into *yes, yes, yes* and become what they dream about?

I feel that the greatest contribution you can make in this world is to grow in self-awareness, self-realization, and the influence to manifest your own personal heartfelt desires and dreams. Of course, the next best thing you can do is to assist others in duplicating what you've done.

It is my ultimate goal that this book will contribute in creating that kind of world for you and for the individuals around you. If it does that, I will have fulfilled my intention of inspiring and influencing you and others to live their lives at their highest level. I can only accomplish this objective by having you commit to educating, training, and implementing the strategies and ideas contained in this book, and by committing to helping me spread the word within your circle of influence.

I have found that the most effective way to master anything is to teach others. Doing so will mentally force you to clarify your ideas, tackle inconsistencies in your own thinking, and then practice what you preach.

This is extremely important because in order to teach others, you will need to read, study, demonstrate, and speak the information over and over again. I'm sure you've heard the saying "Repetition is the mother of learning."

To me, the most rewarding benefit of studying, researching, and teaching people the principles of how to influence is that I'm constantly gaining knowledge. Remember that you are influenced by teaching others how to influence.

The world was not created in one day; therefore, you can't influence everyone in one day. However, if you start the movement by influencing one person and teaching him or her how to influence another person and teaching that person to influence another person, you will see that before you stop and realize, you would have influenced a lot of people. The road to influence is one of the few roads that I have found to always be in construction for perfection.

The key to your success is to influence one person at a time, teaching that person how to duplicate one step at a time. There are many methods you can use to influence others. It can be done via writing, seminars, one-on-one meetings, videos, audio, and any other effective ways you can think of to get your information and point across.

The question that most people ask is, "How can I influence people?" To influence people, you must first get them to listen in order to get your message across—and to make them listen, you must always answer their instinctive questions:

- Why should I listen to you?
- How can I benefit from listening to you?

Once deep listening beings, then you will begin to influence. You will need to keep your listeners motivated at all times in order to make them want to hear more of your story. There are three essential motivating factors that stimulate people to listen to you, and these factors are:

- How do I benefit?
- Who's telling the story?
- How is the story being told?

To assist you in understanding just how influential the above three motivating factors are, let's take a look at ourselves for a moment. What is it that makes us tick? What motivates us to do anything? Keep this in mind that when you lift others up, they in turn lift you up.

Focusing is the key. When you begin to talk, you must focus on your prospective audience, whether it's one-on-one or in a seminar setting, and you will then be answering the basic question of "How do I benefit if I listen to you?"

Who is telling the story is extremely important. Listeners lose control when paying attention because they are letting the speaker take control. It's been proven that paying attention to just anyone is not something people do willingly. Speakers must present trust, respect, value, likeability, openness, and honesty to appeal to the listeners.

So now that you have their undivided attention, how will you tell an effective story? You must first relate to them as an open and real person. What techniques will you use to deliver a compelling message so that people will listen and stay tuned throughout the talk?

Based on my experience, today's audience needs the following elements to pay attention to you. No exceptions! Talk isn't cheap, so make it count.

- You must be clear.
- Have the right topic.
- Have confidence.
- Have an effective opening line to get attention.
- Provide excitement.
- Make your point and then explain.
- Recap your story.
- Have extreme knowledge.
- Sincerely care about your topic and sincerely want to share it with others.
- Have a unique approach.
- Establish credibility with resources and backup data.
- Be passionate.
- Focus on the benefits to the listener.
- Differentiate yourself.
- Have a great reputation.
- Focus on satisfaction.

I encourage you to always think happy—and that will make you feel happy. Act excited about how and what you are presenting and you will become excited. Act with care and you will begin to care!

No matter what business you are working in, I believe influencing other people is all about confidence and the willingness to use yourself to make things happen. Influencing people is about having the ability to work "magic," whether it's in a large seminar setting, a one-on-one meeting, via telephone, a webinar setting, or even when hanging out with your friends and family.

I don't imagine that there is a right or wrong process of influencing people. The key is to influence yourself deeply enough—then you will have the desire and belief to begin to transfer that enthusiasm to others. Your complete behavioral system has to be applied.

We're all influenced by people, places, events, and situations every day. Still, we are mostly influenced by one's surroundings. Therefore, I encourage you to choose your surroundings carefully in order to be positively influenced with the intention of influence others.

The best you can be is the self satisfaction which comes from the feeling of confidence, legitimacy, independence, realization and a feeling of conviction that you are in control of your own future. It is the personal power and energy which you possess within the inner you from accomplishment and assisting others to acomplish.

BE AN
ENTREPRENEUR

Chapter Seventeen

For generations now, we have been taught to go school, get a good education, and be a doctor, lawyer, accountant, teacher, priest, nurse, banker, etc., in order to have a good career. We were taught that working for a large company with insurance benefits and a retirement plan meant living happily ever after. I must say that there is absolutely nothing wrong with having that mentality. In fact, it's often a great idea.

However, there are those who want more than all that security, and they have wondered why no one ever taught them how to become an entrepreneur and enjoy the freedom of being independent. No one explained how to be creative and meet lots of new people. No one explained the challenges and the construction of a road to entrepreneurship, allowing them to reap the rewards of success.

I feel that this is primarily because being an entrepreneur can have its challenges, such as having too much or too little work, playing multiple roles, making initial investments, receiving skepticism and discouragement, etc. However, those who are brave enough to take the entrepreneurial route can earn the opportunity to be an ordinary person with an extraordinary life.

As an entrepreneur, you can be one of those individuals who wake up every morning feeling happy knowing that your day is going to be spent exactly the way you want it to be. You decide if you want to be an employee or an entrepreneur. Personally, I grew up with an entrepreneurial mentality all my life. From a young age, I remember my father having his own business, and I followed his footsteps.

As an entrepreneur, I find that every day is a stimulating new day. I'm always learning exciting new things and opening new doors for greater opportunities.

Even though it can be a rough road in the beginning, I love being an entrepreneur and the excitement of starting and developing a new business. I love the planning, the creativity, the great new people I meet, the execution, the challenges I face, and the potential rewards. Having an entrepreneurial mind-set leaves your options wide open, with absolutely no boundaries. However, it is important for you to get into a business that you understand well, believe in, and are passionate about.

I have started many successful businesses, including a radio program, an actors workshop studio, restaurants, pizzerias, and a production company, and I have been involved in e-commerce, insurance, and investment brokerages, just to name a few. The education and experience I gained was high, yet in retrospect, the journey has been rewarding and worth every bit of my efforts.

What I love most about being an entrepreneur is the day-to-day challenges I go through. Once the business is in motion, I like the challenges of the expansion and the recruiting of new associates to the company to assure stability and growth to the business in order to make it profitable. I enjoy being in the business of duplicating efforts through other people, where I can learn the business well and then teach others how to do it. Assisting others in building their businesses is a great way of building your business, and at the end of the day, it's a win-win situation for all.

An example that I can personally share with you is that when I started to build my life insurance brokerage in 1995, I dedicated myself to learning the licensing manual extremely well, to the point where I was recruiting several people all at once. Then I ran a licensing course for three to four weeks, until they passed their exams and obtained their licences.

Following this, I taught them the sales cycles, showing them the opportunities and providing them with ongoing service, support, and guidance to becoming entrepreneurs. I built a good-sized agency with this method of duplicating efforts through other people. When you believe in yourself, others will believe in you.

There are many reasons someone may want to become an entrepreneur. It could be due to a job loss. Or perhaps a person has been passed over for promotion and there are no opportunities left in the existing business for someone with that particular skill level or interest. Some people are actually repulsed by the idea of working for someone else. On the other hand, some people become entrepreneurs because they are disillusioned by the bureaucracy or politics involved in getting ahead in an established business or profession.

Entrepreneurs are their own bosses and make their own decisions, deciding who they do business with, how hard they will work, how much they get paid, and even when they take vacations.

What I most like about being an entrepreneur is that it also offers a greater possibility of achieving significant financial rewards than working for someone else. Let's take a closer look at some other reasons that someone would want to be an entrepreneur. Doing so involves the following:

- Having the ability to be involved in the total operation of the business, starting with the plan, the
- design, and the implementation process
- The prestige of being the boss
- The opportunity to build your business instead of someone else's; building equity, which has equity or can be passed on to your family
- The opportunity to help the local economy
- Creating job opportunities in your community
- Unlimited income potential

I encourage all people to consider becoming entrepreneurs in order to create their own opportunities instead of having others plan their futures. I haven't met one person who became exceptionally rich from working in a salaried job. All the rich people I have met have been entrepreneurs or people who get a little salary with a significant portion of their income from some sort of override or bonuses based on a production system.

The question that remains is, are you ready to be an entrepreneur? Are you aware of the risks you are likely to face? Do you have what it takes to be a successful entrepreneur? These questions deserve far more serious consideration than they often receive from people interested in getting into business for themselves.

Entrepreneurs have a fundamental position in the economy. Entrepreneurs serve as fuel in our economy's engine, activating and stimulating all economic activity. The most energetic societies in the world are the ones that have the most entrepreneurs, plus the economic and legal structure to encourage and motivate entrepreneurs to do greater activities.

It is important for you to understand the ins and outs of being an entrepreneur. I haven't seen a scripted way to become an entrepreneur, but there are certainly things you can do to make your journey easier.

One encouraging thing is that now some universities and colleges are offering entrepreneurial courses to their students. With the elevated level of unemployment, this is encouraging because our economy can certainly use more people with entrepreneurial mentalities to start up new businesses and create more employment opportunities in our communities.

If you are an entrepreneur in the making, here are some questions to consider before you get started:

- Do you believe in yourself?
- Were you born to be an entrepreneur?
- Do you have a deep, burning desire for more in life?
- Are you creative, energetic, and motivated?
- Do you have a winning strategy?
- Are you passionate?
- Are you disciplined?
- Do you have the hunger for independence?
- Are you a visionary?
- Can you deal with challenges?

- Do you love to learn new things?
- Do you take risks?
- Are you innovative?
- Do you like to meet new people?
- Do you like to help others?
- Do you have integrity, initiative, and innovation?

There are so many other variables that make up a successful entrepreneur. For the most part, these qualities may not be taught; they are either in your genes or they are not. As an entrepreneur, you hold the power of creating your own future, the future you dream of. I know it sounds simple; however, it's definitely not easy.

To be a true entrepreneur, you need to have a certain level of intelligence and love to learn. I have found that if you don't like to learn, your business will not grow—simply because you're not growing. For your business to grow, you must grow along with it because the business's success is at all times directly linked to the success of its owner.

Entrepreneurs are responsible for creating wealth, employment opportunities, and prosperity in our communities and countries. They play a major role in the economy, and we need more entrepreneurs. Do the necessary research, step out of your comfort zone, take a risk if necessary, and start building your own business. You can make a difference if you just believe in yourself. Then others will certainly follow.

This book is not aimed solely at being an entrepreneur; however, it was written by an entrepreneur to share the principles of unleashing the magnet within you and to provide you with ideas that you can begin to implement immediately. To become a leading entrepreneur, you must train yourself to be self-disciplined, focused, and the kind of individual who gets intrinsically motivated to make excellent decisions and take action.

> I learned that courage was not the absence of fear, but the triumph over it. The brave man is not he who does not feel afraid, but he who conquers that fear. *Nelson Mandela*

CHAPTER
EIGHTEEN

F A M O U S
Q U O T E S   F O R
I N S P I R A T I O N

Chapter Eighteen

For as long as I can remember, I have dedicated my life to educating, training, and implementing. I have read and studied many motivational and inspirational books and magazines; watched and listened to a library of videos, tapes, and CDs; and attended countless seminars and workshops. Day in and day out, I have done my best to practice and implement what I have learned.

I have been fortunate enough to have the opportunity to inspire my clients, family, friends, and associates. I have also been fortunate to have the opportunity to use my high level of enthusiasm to inspire and transform thousands of individuals in my keynote presentations, writing, workshops, and videos.

There are many inspirational quotes that I have paid close attention to in my life, and in the following pages, I will share some of them with you. These quotes are inspirational and will add positive thoughts to your day. Reflecting on the words in these quotes can help you change your thoughts. Inspire yourself and inspire others who may need a little lifting up or are having a difficult time and need a little encouragement.

You may already be familiar with some of these quotes and the authors, and some authors you may have never heard of before. However, they have all inspired me. In return, I have shared their inspirational words with others. I hope you will also find some of them inspirational and utilize them in your daily life and business, just as I have done. Good luck!

- One is the number to beat; all the other numbers have been beaten. *Don Xavier*

- When you think you're Remarkable and behave remarkably, others will see you as if you are. *Don Xavier*

- In essence, if we want to direct our lives, we must take control of our consistent actions. It's not what we do once in a while that shapes our lives, but what we do consistently. *Tony Robbins*

- I believe that being successful means having a balance of success stories across the many areas of your life. You can't truly be considered successful in your business life if your home life is in shambles. *Zig Ziglar*

- If you take responsibility for yourself, you will develop a hunger to accomplish your dreams. *Les Brown*

- Every human has four endowments: self-awareness, conscience, independent will, and creative imagination. These give us the ultimate human freedom—the power to choose, to respond, to change. *Stephen Covey*

- It's better to hang out with people better than you. Pick out associates whose behavior is better than yours and you'll drift in that direction. *Warren Buffett*

- Let us all take more responsibility, not only for ourselves and our families but for our communities and our country. *William J. Clinton*

- For Africa to me … is more than a glamorous fact. It is a historical truth. No man can know where he is going unless he knows exactly where he has been and exactly how he arrived at his present place. *Maya Angelou*

- Only one who devotes himself to a cause with his whole strength and soul can be a true master. For this reason mastery demands all of a person. *Albert Einstein*

- Do you want to know who you are? Don't ask. Act! Action will delineate and define you. *Thomas Jefferson*

- Our problems are man-made; therefore, they may be solved by man. And man can be as big as he wants. No problem of human destiny is beyond human beings. *John F. Kennedy*

- Change will not come if we wait for some other person or some other time. We are the ones we've been waiting for. We are the change that we seek. *Barack Obama*

- Watch your thoughts; they become your words. Watch your words; they become your actions. Watch your actions; they become your habits. Watch your habits; they become your character. Watch your character; it becomes your destiny. *Anonymous*

- The ultimate measure of a man is not where he stands in moments of comfort and convenience, but where he stands at times of challenge and controversy. *Martin Luther King, Jr.*

- Your goals are the road maps that guide you and show you what is possible for your life. *Les Brown*

- I was forced to be an artist and a CEO from the beginning, so I was forced to be like a businessman because when I was trying to get a record deal, it was so hard to get a record deal on my own that it was either give up or create my own company. *Jay-Z*

- You've got to follow your passion. You've got to figure out what it is you love—who you really are. And have the courage to do that. I believe that the only courage anybody ever needs is the courage to follow your own dreams. *Oprah Winfrey*

- Everything you are against weakens you. Everything you are for empowers you. *Wayne Dyer*

- You become what you think about and *act* upon. *Don Xavier*

- Be thankful for what you have; you'll end up having more. If you concentrate on what you don't have, you will never, ever have enough. *Oprah Winfrey*

- All mankind is divided into three classes: those that are immovable, those that are movable, and those that move. *Benjamin Franklin*

- I like thinking big. If you're going to be thinking anything, you might as well think big. *Donald Trump*

- I've missed more than 9000 shots in my career. I've lost almost 300 games. Twenty-six times I've been trusted to take the game-winning shot and missed. I've failed over and over and over again in my life. And that is why I succeed. *Michael Jordan*

- I believe that if you show people the problems and you show them the solutions, they will be moved to act. *Bill Gates*

- If you are going to achieve excellence in big things, you develop the habit in little matters. Excellence is not an exception it is a prevailing attitude. *Colin Powell*

- I challenge you to make your life a masterpiece. I challenge you to join the ranks of those people who live what they teach, who walk their talk. *Tony Robbins*

- We have no predictive abilities or control over global trends, natural disasters, political upheavals, currency fluctuation and devaluation, social unrest, bad weather or manic-depressive stock markets. We do, however, have complete control over our own behavior. *Michael Lee-Chin*

- It's the repetition of affirmations that leads to belief. And once that belief becomes a deep conviction, things begin to happen. *Muhammad Ali*

- You are your greatest asset. Put your time, effort, and money into training, grooming, and encouraging your greatest asset. *Tom Hopkins*

- I believe that in order to be successful, you must have a high level of confidence, the courage to execute your plans while being extremely disciplined, and focus on maintaining a winning *I believe* attitude. *Don Xavier*

- The essence of competitiveness is liberated when we make people believe that what they think and do is important—and then get out of their way while they do it. *Jack Welch*

- All successful people, men and women, are big dreamers. They imagine what their future could be, ideal in every respect, and then they work every day toward their distant vision, that goal or purpose. *Brian Tracy*

- Develop an attitude of gratitude, and give thanks for everything that happens to you, knowing that every step forward is a step toward achieving something bigger and better than your current situation. *Brian Tracy*

- A business has to be involving, it has to be fun, and it has to exercise your creative instincts. And obviously, from our own personal point of view, the principal challenge is a personal challenge. *Richard Branson*

- There are a lot of things that go into creating success. I don't like to do just the things I like to do. I like to do things that cause the company to succeed. I don't spend a lot of time doing my favorite activities. *Michael Dell*

- I've been blessed to find people who are smarter than I am, and they help me to execute the vision I have. *Russell Simmons*

- The ability to concentrate and to use your time well is everything if you want to succeed in business—or almost anywhere else for that matter. *Lee Iacocca*

- There are two things to aim at in life: first, to get what you want; and after that, to enjoy it. Only the wisest of mankind has achieved the second. *Logan Pearsall Smith*

- You are accountable for the writing of your personal storybook. How do you want today's page to read? You can shape your destiny! Your actions today will determine your outcome tomorrow. *Don Xavier*

- Nothing can stop the man with the right mental attitude from achieving his goal; nothing on earth can help the man with the wrong mental attitude. *Thomas Jefferson*

- All men dream but not equally. Those who dream by night in the dusty recesses of their minds wake in the day to find that it was vanity; but the dreamers of the day are dangerous men, for they may act their dream with open eyes, to make it possible. *T. E. Lawrence*

- Our destiny changes with our thoughts; we shall become what we wish to become, do what we wish to do, when our habitual thoughts correspond with our desires. *Orison Swett Marden*

- Destiny is not a matter of chance; but a matter of choice. It is not a thing to be waited for; it is a thing to be achieved. *William Jennings Bryan*

- Live your life with passion and build a legacy. *Don Xavier*

- Every time you smile at someone, it is an action of love, a gift to that person, a beautiful thing. *Mother Teresa*

In my own characterization, I have found that your level of inspiration is the same or very similar to your level of vision. Is inspiration tangible? Is inspiration something we do, see, hear, taste, or smell? Is it something any of your five senses can perceive?

All of us become inspired differently. Some individuals are inspired by reading an inspirational book, and some are inspired by attending a seminar and listening to a motivational speaker, while others are inspired by nature, their parents, their children, their friends, a good movie, a favorite song, etc.

What inspires you? Find whatever or whomever inspires and animates you to do the things you enjoy and love doing. As for where you can find inspiration, it can actually come from the unlikeliest source like reading blogs, magazines, brainstorming, theatre, dreams, history, music and forums, just to name a few. Just look at your surroundings and decide what inspiration is in store for you. Inspiration can be found just about everywhere. Allow yourself to open your eyes and heart to recognize it and make a decision to follow it.

This universe can provide everything for you. However, if you're waiting for it to strike you like a bad accident, it will never happen. I suggest that you rely on yourself and kick-start your search to find the things and people who will inspire you and lead you onto the trail to your destiny.

It's a wonderful and stimulating feeling when your heart glides and your soul is moved. After all, inspiration is that very thing that makes you pursue your lifelong dreams. I just can't say it enough; you become what you think about and act upon. Always live your life with passion and build a legacy.

MOTIVATE
YOURSELF AND
INSPIRE
YOUR KIDS

Chapter Nineteen

The children are the future, and if we want our children to play a significant role in the future, then we must motivate ourselves in order to inspire them to be the very best they can be. We must lead by example and walk our talk.

To clarify, no matter what a parent may be—a doctor, accountant, entrepreneur, manager, insurance broker, chef, factory worker, waste management worker, or construction worker—his child is likely to follow in his footsteps and have the same or a similar career.

No matter what your situation or career/job is, you must motivate yourself and inspire your kids by giving them a positive upbringing filled with encouragement, support, love, understanding, and hopes and dreams of a brighter tomorrow.

My daughter Rosilda was about three or four years old when I used to subscribe to Anthony Robbins' Power Talk audio tapes. While I was driving, I'd listen to educational and motivational tapes in the car; and my daughter, well, had no other choice but to listen along with me.

I clearly remember her asking me questions like, "So, Daddy, what is power talk?" I would answer, "Power talk is like a vitamin for your mind, and by listening, learning, and implementing the ideas, you will grow to be a very strong and healthy minded young lady." I don't believe that at the age of three or four, she clearly understood what I meant; however, she knew what vitamins were and what purpose they served because she took them daily.

My daughter and I have always been close and have completed many projects together over the years. She's currently nineteen years old and in her second year of University, studying commerce and majoring in marketing, and we are still working together.

I wonder why! You think it has anything to do with her dad being in some sort of marketing all his life? Do you think it may have to do with all the self-help and motivational tapes and CDs we enjoyed together? Do you think it may have something to do with Mom and Dad being motivated and inspired throughout their lives? Or maybe it's because of genetics that she wants to be a businesswoman and a leader? I don't know for sure, but the point I'm making is that when we try to be the very best we can be, it transfers to our kids because our kids emulate us.

Don't procrastinate. Make a conscious decision that you will be accountable every step of the way, and that you will achieve the necessary knowledge to truly motivate you and inspire your kids to take action.

Staying motivated takes great effort; our drive is continuously being beaten down by negative thoughts and worries about our future and the future of our kids. This is normal for everyone; what truly distinguishes the highly successful is possessing the ability to always shake off the negative thoughts and worries and move ahead.

There is no easy solution for lack of motivation. Even the most motivated individual will lack motivation at times, especially when things don't go as planned. The secret is to understand your thoughts and how they steer your emotions. It is important that you learn how to nurture motivating thoughts, throw away the negative thoughts, and put the task at hand in the spotlight. Make sure that you don't stay in a slump for too long, as you don't want the negativity to get a chance to gain momentum and transfer to your kids.

Being motivated is a lifestyle, either you have learned or created this lifestyle. It has to become a recipe for you to utilize on a daily basis in order to be able to transfer enthusiasm to your kids and others in your life. You're probably thinking that it's not realistic to expect someone to always be up and maintain a yes-yes-yes attitude 24-7, and you're right. However, you do have control of your twenty-four hours per day. Make the best of them.

All the parents I know want to inspire their kids; however, parents need a little reminder that one of the best ways you can educate your kids is to lead by example. And since you are reading this book, I'm certain that you are the sort of individual who wants the very best for your family today, tomorrow, and forever.

Knowledge is wealth. Applied knowledge is power. Therefore, let's explore some effective behaviors and actions that will help inspire your kids:

- Encourage your children to express their opinions.
- Talk about their feelings and teach them to make choices.
- Demonstrate enthusiasm for your children's interests.
- Encourage your children to explore subjects that fascinate them.
- Encourage them to get involved in an organization like Junior Achievement.

- Provide them with play opportunities that support different types of learning.
- Teach them new things with enthusiasm
- Each day, ask what they are learning in school and whether they learned anything new that day.
- Celebrate their grades and accomplishments with rewards, compliments, and congratulations.
- Celebrate achievements, no matter how small.
- Help with school projects and assignments in a way that lets them feel in control of the work.
- Focus on strengths, encouraging developing talents.
- Encourage and support their involvement in music, sports, theatre, community work, etc.
- Turn everyday events into learning opportunities.
- Have an incentive program annually for good grades and participation.
- Show your child that you are involved and interested in what they're involved in by attending all events and functions.
- Never miss a parent-teacher conference.
- Participate in "Take Your Child to Work Day."
- Be your child's advocate.
- Cook with your kids.
- Play with your kids.
- Be involved in your children's lives.

I certainly won't pretend to have all the answers. I have one daughter, and my writing is based on things that I have learned and implemented in my own family life through the parenting process. My objective is to be the best parent I can be by maintaining a positive mental attitude and the determination to lead by example to the best of my ability.

I encourage you to live a life of excitement and live it to the fullest, making sure it truly reflects your sense of passion and purpose. Assist your kids in developing their own unique abilities. I believe that every child has the ability to succeed, and parents have the potential to be their kids' role models for learning. When parents participate in their kids' activities, the connections will have a lifelong impact. Before we move to the next section of the book, I want to leave you with a quote that could be applied to positive parenting by Mahatma Gandhi:

Keep your thoughts positive because your thoughts become your words. Keep your words positive because your words become your behaviors. Keep your behaviors positive because your behaviors become your habits. Keep your habits positive because your habits become your values. Keep your values positive because your values become your destiny.

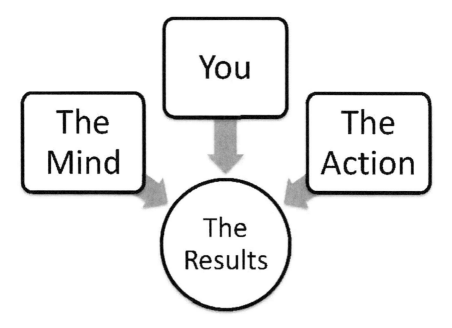

Motivate yourself and inspire your kid(s).

S I G N   A
P L E D G E ,
C O M M I T   T O
Y O U R
S U C C E S S

Chapter Twenty

SIGN A PLEDGE, COMMIT TO YOUR SUCCESS!

I commit

Let's Begin Right Now!

The only regret you may have tomorrow is the regret of not starting today. Today is the beginning of the first day of when all things can come true if you believe and are committed to your personal and professional success.

We have discussed the keys to personal and professional success in previous chapters of this book. In summary, the principles and commitment to your personal and professional success require you to carry out three activities:

- Have complete control of your success.
- Set your goals high.
- Focus and execute until you win—don't give up.

Maintain a positive mental attitude and surround yourself with like-minded people and those who will assist you in making your goals a reality. Achieving success is yours for the taking; it's mine for the taking; and it's available to everyone else who wants it badly enough. As long as we take full responsibility for our actions, then our success is guaranteed because we are the only ones who can create our own reality.

At this point, the key is for you to create your life to be exactly the way you wanted it to be. All it's going to take is your commitment to be persistent and consistent; then you will get to where you want to go. This will not happen in one day, one week, or even one month. The real secret is in having daily actions.

No matter where you are now, your life will change for the better as long as you believe and are fully committed, persistent, and consistent over time. Let's explore some important statements that we must pledge to ourselves in order to guarantee success. I encourage you to read this section of the book as often as you can, reading it for as long as it takes you to memorize it and teach it to others. Better still, have a commitment for breakfast, a commitment for lunch, a commitment for dinner, and if you're still hungry for commitments, have one for a snack.

- I commit to my personal success.
- I commit to all the knowledge necessary to succeed.
- I commit 100 percent to my health and self-image.
- I commit to earning X amount of dollars per year.
- I commit to living in my dream home.
- I commit to meeting with my mentor regularly.
- I commit to driving my dream car.
- I commit to enjoying quality time with my family.
- I commit to working hard and playing hard.
- I commit to living simply—giving more and expecting less.
- I commit to loving more.
- I commit to self-educating, training, and implementing.
- I commit to putting into practice what I preach.

- I commit to relationship building.
- I commit to taking a dream vacation with my family at least once a year.
- I commit to investing at least 10 percent of what I earn.
- I commit to being debt free and having the ability to utilize other people's money.
- I commit to reading industry-related books and articles to help me achieve my goals.
- I commit to attending self-help and business seminars.
- I commit to freeing my mind from worries.
- I commit to letting go of the past.
- I commit to listening to positive affirmation materials in my car.
- I commit to being strong physically, mentally, and spiritually.
- I commit to maintaining a positive outlook on life.
- I commit to honesty.
- I commit to helping people make their dreams a reality.
- I commit to differentiating myself.
- I commit to having a plan and a plan of action.
- I commit to taking actions daily.
- I commit to living to give.
- I commit to my family.

Some of the above commitments may have not existed in your life in the past; however, if you want to get from where you are now to where you want to be, then I encourage you to stay fully committed. In fact, I suggest signing this pledge to your success to remind you daily of your commitments:

I, (your name), commit to all the above commitments, and I promise to read them daily and live by them to the fullest in my life and business.

Keep in mind that committing is the second last step to a more successful you. The final step is to take action and commit to yourself and your road to incredible life-changing success. And remember that the road to success is the only road on which the construction is never truly finished.

You may have other important things that you want to commit to, and I wish you all the best in fulfilling all the above commitments and more.

> The Ultimate Challenge is having the knowledge, the vitality, the ability, and the inspiration to perform at your deepest level in order to establish what you want out of life and ultimately *"take action"* with conviction and gain full control of your destiny!

WRAPPING UP

Chapter Twenty-One

Congratulations! I want to take this opportunity to thank you for reading this book in its entirety. If you have been through all the chapters and completed the self-explorations, you now have an array of proven principles to unleash the magnet within yourself. You are also one of the few with the stamina to face the ultimate challenge, which is taking action.

In this book, I have shared a lot of my own stories, unique styles, determination, and drive to win. Now you have all the necessary powerful tools to allow you to enlarge your vision, make your personal transformation, and apply what you have learned. I certainly trust that you have learned from my research, personal experience, and the behavior that I live by, hoping that you have begun to see the world the way I see it. I see a world where all people can be inspired to truly believe in themselves and their true inner abilities, empowering themselves to attain their full potential and make all their dreams come true.

The foundation of realizing your dreams is clearly understanding how to unleash the magnet within you and possess the Magnetism Effect, a principle that has been passed down from generation to generation.

As I sit here in my backyard feeling the breeze moving through the trees, I'm thinking of how I can conclude this book in a positive way to inspire you to enhance your quality of life and business, leaving you on a soaring note.

Let's take a journey to an imaginary world for a minute. Can you imagine living in a world where everything you dream about can come true and you can live your life to the maximum?

Can you imagine living in a world where you can help others realize their goals and dreams?

Can you imagine living in a world where everything you want can be magnetized to you?

Can you imagine that just by thinking happy thoughts, you will begin to feel happy?

Well, you should start imagining because our actions are guided by our thoughts. You can shape your destiny. Your actions today will determine your outcome tomorrow.

You have abilities and greatness; all you need to do is reach in and bring them out. You have the Magnetism Effect; all you need to do is reach in and bring it out. You can become whatever you think about and *act* upon; all you need to do is boldly venture out of your shadows and become the *you* that you deserve to be!

Develop awareness that to be truly successful you must strive for balance in all areas of your life. The dream for success is alive and kicking for those who are willing to work hard and make their dreams a reality.

Let me say this to you: If you ever decide that you are tired and think of giving up what you are doing, think about looking into the eyes of your family members and saying, "I'm sorry, family. I don't have the guts to win and provide for you anymore." Obviously, this is not an option for you; it's a choice that you never want to make.

My wish is that you will not want to put this book down, that you'll never forget what you've read, and that you'll never lend it to others, instead encouraging them to buy their own copies.

Remember, it's up to you to turn *no, no, no* into *yes, yes, yes* in your life and business, and you can help others do the same. Together we can spread the word to the whole world, one person at a time.

I look forward to receiving your feedback on your Ultimate Challenge in unleashing the magnet in yourself. You can send me your feedback via e-mail at dxavier@donxavier.ca. You can also visit my Web site at www.donxavier.ca.

Until the next time we meet, remember to always be ready to play full out. Last but certainly not least, I wish you the greatest wealth possible: *your health*!

God Bless!

Don Xavier

Throughout this book, I have given you ideas and examples to assist you in making your dreams a reality. The reason I did so is to share with you the principles utilized by successful individuals. Reading this book is the first step; however, reading it alone will not help you make your dreams a reality. *Taking action* is what will make your dreams a reality. By *taking action*, even small action, one step at a time, over a long period of time, you will begin to make positive changes in your life and ultimately make your dreams a reality. Take a close look at where you are now. Evaluate yourself, take the Ultimate Challenge (action), and confidently face your future.

Don Xavier—Biography

Don Xavier was born Agnaldo Lopes Monteiro Xavier in the small town of Piasco, on the Island of Fogo, Cape Verde Islands. In search of the Canadian dream, he immigrated to Canada in 1974. Don successfully completed and graduated high school in 1978—followed by a year off, during which he began taking college-level courses and obtaining certificates in acting, music, and business management. In 1978, Don landed his first television role in the television pilot *Ricky*, which assisted him in earning Union credits and eventually becoming a full member of ACTRA (Alliance of Canadian Cinema, Television, and Radio Artists).

From the late seventies and throughout the eighties and nineties, Don worked in many television and film productions, including *The Final Goal*, *Ricky*, *Top Cops*, *Night Heat*, *Kung Fu: The Legend Continues*, *Johnny Mnemonic*, and *City Sports*, and several TV commercials, industrial training videos, and print advertisements.

Don was also a member of two singing groups right out of high school, and in 1988 he recorded a solo album titled *Dance With Me*, whose song "Princess" gave him recognition in Canada and around the world.

Along with his music and acting career, his entrepreneurial spirit led him to become involved in a pizzeria franchise in 1981. In 1988, he coproduced a radio program called *Rock-in-Stock* (singing most of the commercial jingles for the show). In 1990, he opened another pizzeria, called The Pizza Store. In 1993, he and a partner started The Talent Studio (an actors workshop).

Don started in the financial services industry in 1987 (although he took a break from the industry from 1990 to 1992). His first appointment in the industry was as an agent with a large Canadian insurance company, and with growing success, he progressed to the position of district branch manager.

In 1995, he joined Versatile Financial Group as the general manager of insurance operations, and presently he is the owner-president and CEO. Under his leadership, Versatile Financial Group has gone from twenty-eight representatives in 1996 to over three hundred contracted representatives in 2010.

He knows the life insurance/financial industry inside out, and he has put his knowledge to work in his book *Motivational Cycles to Successful Selling* and his motivational seminars and workshops across North America. Don uses his insider's knowledge to provide readers with the motivation and confidence they need to transform their lives and businesses.

As a speaker and educator, Don is enthusiastic, entertaining, and motivating. His writing and speaking inspire action, and Don's workshops are a moving self-management program for all those who want to shake off mediocrity and live up to their greatness today.

Don is a sought-after and highly rated speaker who has appeared on the Pro-Seminars circuit since 2000. He has spoken at Advocis, Managing General Agencies, Associate General Agencies, Mutual Fund Dealers, many industry events, high schools, MLMs, as well as company sales forces across Canada and the United States.

Don's corporate workshop on how to *Unleash The Magnet In You* ™ will bring a simple yet powerful message to his audiences. The ideas are practical and motivational, and they can immediately be implemented by anyone in any industry.

Don's other credits include movie and television appearances on GREEN, Wild Card, Coping with Hypertension, City Magazine, Lamire, MTV 47, Cabo Video, several TV commercials, infomercials on final expense insurance, and countless radio programs. He has also done advertising print work such as Scotiabank's Mastercard, which was featured throughout the Caribbean. As a singer and songwriter, Don, who currently lives in Canada, has released two albums, *Dance with Me*, *Amor e Evolução and a* Single – "Princess" as well as the music video entitled "Confiança." Don is an active member of ACTRA and SOCAN.

Don's Timeline

1961 – Born in Piasco, Fogo, Cape Verde Islands

1973 – Lived in Portugal

1974 – Immigrated to Canada

1978 – Graduated from high school

1978 – 1980 – Singing groups and television

1981 – Pizza franchise

1982 – 1987 – Acting, music, writing and food industry

1987 – Entered financial services industry

1988 – Release first solo album, Dance with Me, with hit song "Princess"

1988 – Coproduced radio program *Rock-in-Stock*

1990 – Married Maria Xavier
       Opened The Pizza Store

1991 – The best thing that ever happened to him: daughter Rosilda was born

1992 – Released album titled Amor e Evoluc*ã*o

1993 – The Talent Studio (actors workshop) – partner

1999 – Versatile Financial Group – owner-president & CEO

2000 – Began Public Speaking Career

2001 – Manulife Securities – branch owner

2005 – Motivational Cycles to Successful Selling – first book

2007 – Motivational Cycles to Successful Selling – second edition

2009 – Began to build dream home in Santa Maria, Sal, Cape Verde Islands

2010 – Unleash the Magnet in You: The Ultimate Challenge – self-help book

> We all have the same success and failures
>
> We share success when we do something extraordinary.
> We share failure when we quit too soon.
> We're successful when we're the best at what we do.
> We fail the minute we lose focus and take our eyes off our goals and objectives.

Contact

For more information about public speaking, keynote speaking, workshops, retreats, interviews, film, television, or print, please contact me at dxavier@donxavier.ca or visit my Web site: www. donxavier.ca or www.donxavier.com

Mailing address:

Don Xavier
2794 Rainbow Crescent, Mississauga,
Ontario, Canada L5L 5W1

If you've enjoyed reading *Unleash the Magnet in You,*
I invite you to check out my other book: *Motivational Cycles to Successful Selling.*™
To purchase, go to http://www.iuniverse.com/Bookstore/BookDetail.
aspx?BookId=SKU-000113327.

Share *Unleash the Magnet in You*

Who else do you know who needs to unleash the magnet within themselves? Make a list of co-workers, friends, and family members who can benefit from this book. Then show them how to obtain their own copy, buy them one.

_____

_____

_____

_____

_____

_____

_____

_____

_____

Helping others learn how to unleash the magnet within themselves might be the most valuable thing you'll ever do for them.

Thank you for sharing and for the referrals.

Don Xavier

Volume Purchasing

Because this is the type of book that people want to use to train, motivate, and maintain their staff or sales representatives, we will offer you a volume discount if you contact dxavier@donxavier.ca.

Quantity	Discount
10 to 50	10%
51 to 100	15%

Be motivated—make *Unleash the Magnet in You* a lifelong lifestyle.

I trust that you have been inspired by this book; therefore, I recommend that you read my previous book, *Motivational Cycles to Successful Selling* (ISBN: 9781440109003), and learn, live, and do more.

Social Networking

You may also want to follow me daily on the internet:
www.donxavier.ca

Facebook:

www.facebook.com/xavierdon

www.facebook.com/unleashthemagnet

Hi5:

donxavier.hi5.com

Twitter:

www.twitter.com/donxavier1

Myspace:

www.myspace.com/donxavier

YouTube:

www.youtube.com/xavierdon

I would love to hear from you about your experience
with my books, seminars, and workshops.

Recommended Books to Read

The following is a list of recommended books that have played an important role in my life and may enhance your ability to unleash the magnet within you.

Your Personal Best by Mike Lipkin. Toronto, Ontario: Environics/ Lipkin, 2002.

Your Best Life Now by Joel Osteen. New York, New York: Faith Words, 2004.

The Secret by Rhonda Byrne. New York, New York: Atria Books/Beyond Words, 2006.

The E Myth by Michael E. Gerber. New York, New York: HarperCollins, 1995.

Purple Cow by Seth Godin. New York, New York: Portfolio, a member of Penguin Group (USA) Inc., 2003.

The Dip by Seth Godin. New York, New York: Portfolio, a member of Penguin Group (USA) Inc., 2007.

The Richest Man in Babylon by George S. Clason. New York, New York: Signet, an imprint of New American Library, a division of Penguin Group (USA) Inc., 1955.

The Elements of Great Public Speaking by J. Lyman MacInnis. Berkeley, California: Ten Speed Press, 2006.

The Success Principles by Jack Canfield. New York, New York: HarperCollins, 2005.

Why We Want You to be Rich by Donald J. Trump and Robert T. Kiyosaki. New York, New York: Rich Press, 2006.

Something Good's Gonna Happen by Paul Orberson. Georgetown, Kentucky: Hi-Hope Publishing Company, LLC, 2007.

CPSIA information can be obtained at www.ICGtesting.com
Printed in the USA
BVOW082236120713

325725BV00002B/3/P

9 781450 267373